'I came to the House thinking p[...] about money. You decide about the money, and then make the ideas fit.' *Independent*, quoting an anonymous Conservative MP, after the hanging of Farzad Bazoft, 16 March 1990.

'It was the only time he laughed.' Tory MP Robert Adley, who asked Saddam Hussein whether he could see Baghdad's steam engines on a visit to Iraq in February 1988.

'A box of fudge.' Tory MP Richard Page describing a present he received during the same trip.

'There was a plump baby whose face, frozen in a scream, stuck out from under the protective arm of a man, away from the open door of a house that he never reached. Nearby a family of five who had been sitting in their garden eating lunch were cut down – the killer gas not even sparing the family cat or the birds in the tree, which littered the well-kept lawn.' Richard Beeston, *The Times*, on Saddam's gassing of Halabja, 22 March 1988.

'Screwdrivers are also required to make hydrogen bombs' William Waldegrave, Foreign Office minister, approving British technology to Iraq's munitions factories, 6 February 1989.

John Sweeney was the only reporter who covered the Matrix Churchill trial who has also been detained by the Iraqi secret police at a road-block in northern Iraq. With a colleague, he crashed the road-block. Born in 1958, he was educated at grammar school, the LSE and on the Sheffield Telegraph. As an *Observer* journalist, he covered the 1989 revolutions in Eastern Europe. Reporting the Romanian revolution led to *The Life and Evil Times of Nicolae Ceausescu* (London: Hutchinson, 1991), which was reviewed by Jeremy Paxman: 'the horrors of the police state are here in abundance . . . hilarious if they weren't so tragic.'

In former Yugoslavia, he has covered the sieges of Osijek, Dubrovnik, Vukovar and Sarajevo. In Iraq, he has reported on the plight of Saddam Hussein's victims.

Married with one son and one daughter, he lives in London.

TRADING WITH THE ENEMY

HOW BRITAIN ARMED IRAQ

JOHN SWEENEY

A PAN ORIGINAL
PAN BOOKS
LONDON, SYDNEY AND AUCKLAND

First published 1993 by Pan Books Ltd

a division of Pan Macmillan Publishers Limited
Cavaye Place London SW10 9PG
and Basingstoke

Associated companies throughout the world

ISBN 0 330 33128 0

Copyright © John Sweeney 1993

1 3 5 7 9 8 6 4 2

A CIP catalogue record for this book is available from
the British Library

The author and publisher gratefully acknowledge the following for
permission to quote:
Prisoner in Baghdad, Daphne Parish with Pat Lancaster, London:
Chapmans 1992
Saddam's War, John Bulloch and Harvey Morris, London: Faber 1991
Spycatcher: The Candid Autobiography of a Senior Intelligence Officer, Peter Wright,
New York: Viking, 1987
The Death Lobby, Kenneth Timmerman, London: Fourth Estate, 1992
Private Eye: 'The Secret Diary of John Major, aged 47¾, 4 December 1992

Typeset by Cambridge Composing (UK) Limited, Cambridge
Printed by Cox & Wyman Ltd.

ACKNOWLEDGEMENTS

This book would not have been possible without the help or information from a battery of contacts, politicians, fellow journalists and the gang of usual deadbeats who pass for my friends. Some of them did not speak to me personally, but helped by their actions, reports or journalism to cast more light on the murky business of Britain's secret trade with Iraq.

In alphabetical order I would like to thank the following: Robert Adley MP; Dr Dlawer Ala'Aldeen; the staff of Amnesty International; Lord Avebury; John Biffen MP; John Blake of the BBC; Michael Brown MP; Nicholas Budgen MP; John Bulloch of the *Independent*; Alan Clark; Ann Clwyd MP; Robin Cook MP, and in his office Geoffrey Norris and Tom Franklin; John Cummings, MP; Professor J. F. Eastham of Bath University; a cast of thousands on the *Financial Times*, especially Danny Green; Stephen Egerton, former ambassador to Iraq; Jonathan Gebbie, who helped to zap my computer virus; Alan George, the writer on Iraq who unpicked Saddam's secrets long before anyone else; Helga Graham, whose reports on the Iraqi suppression of the Kurds make haunting reading; Dr Omar al-Hassan of the Gulf Centre for Strategic Studies; Dr Alastair Hay of the chemical pathology department of Leeds University who made available his own notes on poison gas victims; Robert Hicks MP; Mark Higson, formerly of the Foreign Office Iraq desk; the indefatigable journalist Mark Hollingsworth; the Insight team at the *Sunday Times*; David Leigh of *This Week* for his stimulus; Martin Leigh; Ken Livingstone MP; Mike Malyon of the Bedworth and Nuneaton *Herald and Post*; Tony Marlow MP; Roger Moate MP; Harvey Morris of the

ACKNOWLEDGEMENTS

Independent; the staff of Newgate Reporters; Richard Norton-Taylor of the *Guardian*; Bertie Odone; Toby Odone and Aimey Jaffe of *Petroleum Intelligence Weekly*; the *Panorama* team who investigated the Matrix Churchill story; Richard Page MP; Robert Parry MP; Alex Patel; Alan Patterson; Gwynne Roberts who made available to the author his hard evidence of Iraq's use of poison gas; Roth's *Parliamentary Profiles*; James Rusbridger; Kim Sengupta of the *Daily Star*; Liz and William Sigmund of the Working Party on Chemical and Biological Weapons; John Steel of the *Daily Telegraph*; Barbara Sweeney; Leonard Sweeney; Steven Thornton; Kenneth R. Timmerman, whose book *Death Lobby* (London: Fourth Estate, 1992) was a constant source of reference; Paul Vickers of Granada Television; David Young MP.

A number of people helped me who required anonymity. To those: silent thanks.

I wish to single out two researchers who helped me solve various riddles: Liz Miller, of the London School of Economics, and Alice Pitman, the freelance journalist.

At the *Observer* I am in debt to the following: my editor Donald Trelford, his deputy Adrian Hamilton and news editor David Randall, my colleagues Martin Bailey, Ruth Fisher, Julie Flint, Jane Renton, Sarah Whitebloom. Special thanks are due to Peter Beaumont and John McGhie. I must thank Peter McFadyen who zapped the computer virus. Every *Observer* journalist is in debt to the staff of the library, Jeffrey Care, Scott Harrison, Millie Pollard and June Sirc. I would also like to mention my friend Andrew Billen, for his constant help and unstinting encouragement.

My agent, Derek Johns, and my publishers, Ian Chapman and Catherine Hurley at Pan Books helped guide me through various minefields.

The greatest thanks of all is due to Anne Patterson.

Trading with the Enemy is written in memory of three journalists who helped shine some truth on the story: Farzad Bazoft, hanged by the Iraqis; Paul Jenks, killed by unknown hand in Croatia; John Merritt, who died of cancer.

The book is dedicated to my son, Sam.

INTRODUCTION

This is a story not about lies and the art of lying but about truth and the art of refining the truth. It is a story about a secret trade with a tyrant so ugly that no Cabinet minister cared to defend it. It is a story that turns on words and the twisting of words: trade and lethality; honesty and expediency; commerce and atrocity; economy and execution. The narrative takes us on a great paper chase, into the secret heart of the British Government. Once within this shadowland of ambiguity, can anyone – prime ministers, ministers, civil servants, arms dealers, spies – be trusted?

It is murky and muddy and, at times, extremely complicated. But to understand Iraqgate is not that difficult. Imagine a set of Russian *matryoshka* dolls, fitting snugly one underneath another. Imagine the smooth blank faces of the dolls, John Major, Margaret Thatcher, Tony Newton, David Mellor . . . They and many more have a part to play in the secret trade with Iraq. And beneath them, the final doll. There it is, with a thick moustache and a chilling smile.

The Father of the Iraqi nation.

Each doll knew part of the truth, that Britain traded with Saddam Hussein; each doll knew something of the arms embargo that never was; each doll played a part in defending the trade; some took part in the cover-up which aimed to prevent that secret entering into the public domain.

There is one fixed point in the story of Britain's secret

arming of Saddam: the awesome malevolence of the Iraqi regime. In the spring of 1991, I saw this evil with my own eyes.

In the thickening light at the foot of a mountain pass we reached them, a mudslide made of people, and handed them their first Western aid: not blankets or food or medicine, but bubblegum. A two-year-old clutched the little cylinder of Milka Chew, wrapped in a brown and yellow packet showing a wolf chasing a piccaninny, as if it was something magical. The left side of her face was blistered with infection – frostbite? – swollen with pus which needed immediate hospital treatment. Easy in the West; not so if the child is one of six lying in the back of a trailer pulled by a tractor, itself stuck in a monstrous traffic jam.

Even in the dark one could sense, rather than see, that the mountain road was dense with humanity. Flickering fires threaded away, up, up, up and out of view. In the next trailer a baby, barely a day old, slept. Then came a family huddled, sleeping in a taxi painted in the distinctive orange and white Iraqi colours, and then a mobile crane, its platform the al fresco home of twelve children and six adults; then a lorry, again crammed with people. In the flashlight a mother moved and unpicked a bundle, unwrapping it to show a baby, naked, blue and so still it seemed that even what small or fatuous aid we could offer would be of no use.

In the morning, the monstrousness of what Saddam had done to the Kurds uncoiled before us as far as the eye could see and beyond. The snow-capped mountain pass on the Iran–Iraq border, on the road from Halabja, was strewn with thousands upon thousands of people. I had never seen such exhaustion.

You could only take in so much misery before switching off. It was wretched to see one mother hold her toddler as he squatted and squirted bile yellow diarrhoea by the side of the road. After the tenth such scene it became almost commonplace. Soon the puddles of yellow shit were just part of the landscape.

So many hundreds of thousands had fled Saddam's revenge

after the failure of their uprising, following Iraq's expulsion from Kuwait, that the Iranian army had blocked the border, letting people into safety in ones and twos. The Iranian soldiers had brought the pace of the traffic to a virtual stop by a bridge over the surging river Sirwan, leaving families trapped in a motor-bound refugee camp. The poor who came on foot or in buses were in a happier state in the tent city which lined the other bank. The better-off, fearful of losing their vehicles, were trapped by their own comparative riches in the jam.

But that was not to say that life in the tent city was good. The journey over the mountains was too harsh for that, the danger of infectious diseases in this press of sick people too great. One hard-pressed Iranian doctor, Sadeq Nemati, gestured at three tents near by: 'Welcome to my hospital.'

There was an understocked pharmacy, and only one drip for the 4600 people in that patch of hillside. The worst problems were caused by dehydration and amoebic dysentery. In the past week, he said, ten children under the age of one had died from a combination of these two killers. A little cemetery overlooking the camp with some small, freshly dug graves gave sharp meaning to the statistics.

In the camp it proved a mistake to hand out in public our bubblegum, biscuits and chocolate: the children would look enviously at the lucky ones, triggering small-scale versions of the adult food riots that started the moment the Iranian bread truck arrived. We learnt to palm the sticks of Milka Chew as if they were baksheesh.

The sight of grown men rising and falling like fish-farm trout at feeding time was striking and upsetting the first time. But after, say, thirty times in the same day one's sense of shame gave way to an uneasy, shifty boredom.

No one contested five-year-old Khaled Sadiq's claim to his bubblegum. All the Milka Chews in the world would not make up for what Saddam's men did to his face, which looked like a bowl of burnt porridge. Napalm? No. One of the American journalists who had covered Vietnam recognized the distinctive features of a phosphorus burn. The Iraqis used phosphorus bombs as markers, so that more conventional explosives would find their target. The bomb had been dropped from an Iraqi helicopter gunship when he and his family were at his home in Kirkuk twenty days before. His eyes looked out from his blisters and gazed at his Milka Chew. The bubblegum had made his day.

How could the Iraqis have got away with bombing civilians, after their signal defeat in Kuwait? The answer: Saddam was as cunning as he was cruel. After the Iraqis had been thrown out of Kuwait, General Norman Schwarzkopf had banned Iraqi jets from the skies, but permitted helicopter flights, bowing to special pleading that the regime needed to drop 'insecticide' on marshland to counter malarial mosquitoes. Subsequently, the general admitted that he had been 'suckered'. The burnt porridge face was the visible evidence of the error of taking the Iraqis at their word.

The traffic jam packed the road all the way to the border crossing. It was endless, hot and dusty at noon, freezing at midnight. It became so long that only the really remarkable vehicles merited a comment. A brightly coloured combine harvester, absurd among the snowy mountains with a vicious drop inches from its wheels. Further on a Cutlass Sierra Oldsmobile, a refugee from an American TV detective show like *Kojak*, were it not cluttered with Kurds.

You could still see the artillery damage the Iraqis had wrought on the hillside villages during the Iran-Iraq war. The shellholes were a novelty, more arresting than the crush of people, the shitting toddlers and the rash of food riots as the food trucks went by.

The border was a disappointment. There was no let up in the jam; some refugees said that it continued back into Iraq as far as forty miles. Not far down the road was the town of Halabja, which Saddam gas-bombed in 1988, killing 5000 Kurds. Several people from Halabja were in the jam, many delighted to meet an Englishman. Had they known that later that year, after their town was gassed, the British government sent a minister, Tony

Newton, now leader of the House of Commons, to Baghdad to sell to the killers, they may not have been quite so courteous.

It was not possible to go into Iraq then. Our Iranian minders would not let us go further. Besides, it was difficult to take in the innocent meadows and mountains of Iraq without sensing a brooding menace.

The Kurds told us countless versions of the same story: how they fled from the towns of northern Iraq, Kirkuk, Sulaimaniya, Halabja, at the sound of shelling, or the appearance of the gunships. How Saddam had butchered their relatives, gouging out eyes, murdering children.

Much of what they said sounded exaggerated. The exodus had something in common with the reaction of the Americans when Orson Welles produced his too-lifelike *War of the Worlds* on the radio in the thirties – a mass psychosis. But then you remembered Halabja, the fate of executed *Observer* reporter Farzad Bazoft and the face of the little boy blinking at his bubblegum and you knew that not all the atrocity stories had been made up.

It was all the more upsetting because these kids could have been your own children. It was unbearably affecting.

Anything we could give to make up for the suffering seemed better than nothing, even bubblegum and dry biscuits. But sometimes even this parody of Western aid went wrong. On our trip back from the border a colleague, a decent fellow, lobbed a packet of biscuits out of the window of the speeding bus at a family nestled by the roadside around a plastic shack. The gift smashed into the face of a little girl, who burst into tears. And then the scene vanished, as the bus hurried on . . .

But something better than bubblegum arrived a few days later. There were echoes of *Apocalypse Now* as junior Foreign Office minister Mrs Lynda Chalker, on a helicopter 'PR bullship', swooped down on the mountain meadow marking the Iran–Iraq border.

The local director of the United Nations High Commissioner for Refugees, Omar Bakhat, had declared that week that the situation of the Kurds in Iran was 'total chaos'. So what better way to help feed, clothe and nurse the Kurds than a 'fact-finding' mission by a minister?

Her Majesty's Government had pulled out all the stops, which meant borrowing a jet of the Queen's flight and then hitching a ride on an Iranian air force Chinook chopper.

The border photo-opportunity had a fine background of gleaming snow in the sunshine, but was marred by the presence of several thousand Kurdish men trapped on the Iraqi side, just behind two strands of barbed wire and menaced by Iranian soldiers. (The Iranians, knocked back by the million-strong wave of people, had by now closed their borders.) Behind the wire, the Kurds looked like POWs.

Mrs Chalker walked over to the barbed wire, gamely announcing that the border was open. The Kurds, nearly all men, pressed against the barbed wire as if to prove that the border was anything but. Mrs Chalker moved away. There were few English speakers in the throng. One man started to speak grimly about the conditions for his family, trapped on the wrong side of the border. This wasn't the right sort of image. A Foreign Office minder stepped in: 'The pilot wants to go.'

The PR bullship took off again, landing in a refugee camp near by. Mrs Chalker headed off towards the tent city, surrounded by a crush of Kurds, who were kept back by a man brandishing a stick. The minister stumbled across an empty aid box. She stopped dead and read the label. Was it British? 'Austrian,' she said. A man stopped her: 'Where is food?' She replied: 'We have already sent food.' The Kurd looked at her in disbelief.

The minister carried on: 'We have all sent aid, the British, the Americans, the French and the Dutch.' 'Where is the Dutch?' asked the sceptical Kurd. 'It's a small country in Europe,' she said and then moved on. Another Kurd shouted in German: 'Essen – nicht haben.' ('Nothing to eat.') The minister said: 'We are giving you three million water purification tablets.' Aid workers later pointed out that the Kurds have no containers in which to purify the water.

A Kurdish doctor who had fluent English yelled: 'Where is George Bush's humanity?' The crush swirled into a tent, a mother and baby appearing in the gloom. But the baby had diarrhoea and the ministerial presence moved on. We choppered over to a second camp. A Kurd shouted: 'We need clean water. All children is sick for water.' The minister told him about the purification tablets. Where were they? In Oroumiyeh, two hours by road from the camps, a road which the Kurds were not allowed to travel down.

There were chants of 'Death to Saddam' and, curiously, 'Viva François Mitterrand', raising the suspicion that the Kurds were guilty of mistaken identity. Another Kurd shouted: 'Four children have died today', but one of the Foreign Office minders had, by now, found a fit, healthy-looking baby. The minister hugged the baby, saying: 'We have to make sure that this child and all the others will live.'

The chopper roared again, and the minister (now Lady Chalker) looked on as the Kurds on the mountainside shrank, diminished into dots, and then disappeared.

Hundreds of miles to the south, in the prickly heat of the Persian Gulf, it was sobering to talk to Arabs wearing *djellaba* saying precisely the same things about Saddam as the Kurds: that he was a monster, that his men shelled and bombed their homes, that they feared their brothers and sisters were dead.

These refugees were Iraqi Shias, whose rebellion against Saddam had also collapsed and who had fled to the Paul Nash Sommescape of shell-holes around the shattered city of Khorramshahr.

One thirty-year-old man, too frightened to give his name, proffered a burnt hand in a dirty bandage. He, too, had been blasted by a phosphorus bomb, dropped from one of Saddam's 'insecticide' gunships.

In the south it was not the cold but the heat that was the enemy of the refugees. Even in mid-April, the sun scoured down on the tent city. The scale of the Shias' misery was less dramatic, less photogenic than the Kurds, but the fear was just as great. When a Western television crew started to film a busload of women and children who had just made it across the marshes to the safety of Iran, the women hid their faces; one wept uncontrollably.

Iraq itself was grim indeed.

It was the smell that first alerted the Americans to what might be under the dusty earth of the barrack gardens. That, and shallow bumps under one US Marine Corps tent. They moved the tents and started to dig. They found a scalp, bones and 'sneakers' to fit a three-year-old. Then they stopped digging, covered up the earth and poured diesel to hide the sour-sweet stench of decay.

But what the Americans had stumbled on was no public cemetery. The bodies were found in the barrack gardens of the 44th Division of the Iraqi army. These graves were secret, not a mile from the town cemetery. Kurds try to bury their dead with dignity, even in the mountains. Perhaps they held good forensic evidence of what Amnesty International has long reported, that Saddam's men routinely torture and execute children in front of their parents.

Creepy? 'I come from Bangor, Maine, where Stephen King lives,' said US Sergeant Frank Jordan as he stepped down from his Humvee, one of the first United Nations troops into Northern Iraq to clear out Saddam's men and set up a safe haven for the Kurds. 'This is like one of his novels. It's like *It*.'

The sergeant had just arrived in Zakho, a dusty town in Kurd-populated northern Iraq near the Turkish and Syrian borders, which was still under Saddam's control. US Marines passed knots of Iraqi troops in bottle green standing on street corners.

Conversations would start in a shop, in broken English, then stop in mid-sentence as a well-groomed stranger wandered in. Everywhere one went, one was watched. There is watching and watching, of course. Some watching is just good-natured nosiness. This watching was pregnant with unease.

Down a whitewashed side street a black-clad priest scuttled from his church. He saw us and offered, 'Hello.' But his eyes were elsewhere, watching two men in jeans and T-shirts watching him. The priest vanished like a spider down a hole. One of the secret policemen, the Mukhabarat, smiled at us, the smile of an enemy.

Suddenly, the troops and the Mukhabarat had gone, back to Baghdad, leaving the police station as Saddam's last outpost. The Kurds struck at nightfall, lobbing a hand grenade into its porch.

The injured, two Iraqi policemen, squealed like piglets as they came into a field hospital run by French medics. One had been badly wounded in the leg and was letting the world know about it. The sight of any human pain is always distressing, made more so by the bloodless face lit by torchlight – there was no electricity. Yet, having seen so much suffering caused by killers much like the policeman, there was something satisfactory about his pain. The ugliness of this thought kept me from sleep.

The following morning I went into the deserted police station, examined the trail of blood left the night before by the injured policeman. A handprint of blood patterned the length of a wall. Upstairs, in the commander's empty office, hung an enormous photograph of Saddam in Kurdish dress. I unhooked it from the wall and let it go. In the stillness of the early morning it made a satisfying smash.

Saddam's men on the run and the comforting presence of American firepower made one too confident. One day John Pomphret, a reporter from Associated Press, and I risked a ride beyond the safe haven into Dahuk in Saddam's Iraq. We met a blind Kurdish student, who had just returned from the mountains. His useless eyes flickered this way and that as he listed what they had stolen. They had taken his two violins, an electronic organ, a television, a telephone, clothes, an air-conditioning unit, a specially crafted chess set with grooves for the pieces, two touch watches, dozens of cassettes he used for study. They had smashed his photograph hanging on the wall. And they had stolen his braille books, even his braille Koran.

He showed us around his bedroom. I photographed him as his fingers searched in vain for his guitar where it used to hang on a nail. It was his first day back, and the realization that not only everything valuable but also everything which helped him overcome his blindness had gone made him weep. The photograph of the blind man weeping would have been striking, but he became worried that they might take revenge and asked us not to use the photographs or to name him. Such was the fear of Saddam.

On the journey back, we got stuck at a checkpoint, manned by the Iraqis.

'Visa for Iraq?' The question did not come from an ordinary soldier but from a plain-clothes Mukhabarat man in mirror shades and the conventional villain's pitted face.

'No,' said Pomphret, at the wheel.

'Switch the engine off.' On my side of the jeep was a fat Iraqi holding a rifle. He looked up, like a bull beginning to take notice.

'Switch it off.'

'OK.'

If we surrendered to them, the chances were good that we would be escorted to Baghdad, where the last *Observer* reporter there had been hanged, after torture.

'Switch it off.'

'I said OK.' Instead Pomphret gunned the car, and we roared off, heads shrinking into our necks. Seconds passed. They didn't shoot us. Perhaps they had had a surfeit of killing.

At the US checkpoint, a Marine said: 'I don't know why they didn't let us go get him when we wanted to,' and spat mightily in the dust.

The evidence of Saddam's evil was abundant, had been so ever since he used chemical weapons against the Iranian troops in the mid-eighties, an outrage which caused the British government to draw up guidelines to stop arms-trading with Iraq. Throughout, the British government appeared to lead the world in its condemnation of Saddam's abuses of human rights. Lady Chalker's visit was part and parcel of our government's official policy: humane, civilized, an enemy of tyranny.

But running parallel to this official condemnation was a confidential accommodation, in which Saddam was prized as a much-valued customer. The effect of bending the guidelines and furthering trade credits to Saddam's Iraq was that our government bolstered his savagery. Ministers were made accessories to his genocide. After the invasion of Kuwait, some did their best to cover up the story of the secret trade with Iraq, even at the expense of risking the liberty of three British businessmen. The machinery of Westminster and Whitehall girded itself to stop the truth coming out: that Her Majesty's Government traded with the enemy.

CHAPTER
ONE

'Not Guilty!'

Pop! Fizz! Splutter!

The squirting of champagne to symbolize victory has now become part of the ritual of British justice, as well established in the overpriced pantomime as the lawyers' wigs, the muttered m'luds and the oath on the Holy Book. The bottle of bubbly had materialized from somewhere, the glasses handed out by solicitor Kevin Robinson with the self-effacing smoothness of Bertie Wooster's Jeeves. The Matrix Churchill Three – Trevor Abraham, Peter Allen and Paul Henderson – waited expectantly for the *pop!* on the pavement outside the Old Bailey.

Pop! It was a disappointingly quiet *pop!* in the event, virtually drowned out by the roar of London's traffic. Perhaps, for some of the ministers who might have favoured a different verdict, it was more like a muffled shot. But the opening of the champagne bottle, the fizz of good French wine and the time-honoured ritual of a toast all provided essential 'visuals' for the photographers and cameramen jockeying for position. The camera shutters clicked and the TV tapes whirred. But soft *pop!* though it might have been it triggered a set of explosions across London, Britain, the Western world, all the way to the old, valued customer back in Baghdad.

Pop! The jury's not guilty verdict sent a *galère* of government ministers scurrying for cover. BBC Radio Four's *PM* programme that night could find not one senior government player to explain their case. Embarrassment all around at the Palace of Westminster.

Pop! Things were no better in Whitehall, where a battery of civil servants started reading their own most secret minutes on the arms trade with Iraq, urging utmost secrecy, as they tucked into their morning newspapers over breakfast. For example, it is unlikely that senior civil servant at the Department of Trade and Industry (DTI), Michael Coolican, ever intended this angst-ridden whinge to see the light of day, written on 14 June 1990, a few weeks before the invasion of Kuwait to his secretary of state Nicholas Ridley: 'The dirty washing liable to emerge from the action proposed by Customs and Excise will add to the problems caused by the supergun. For the DTI the timing is extraordinarily embarrassing.' And how . . .

Pop! Dismay at the ghastly glass and concrete shoe-box headquarters of MI5, near Euston, because the evidence of one of their officers in the trial had done much to destroy the Crown's case.

Pop! Anxiety within the even more hideous block of offices near the Imperial War Museum, the home of MI6, because the service had appeared to abandon one of its most valued agents, defendant Paul Henderson, despite testimony from an MI6 officer at the trial that 'he was a very brave man'.

Over the next few days there followed a fantastic media-feeding frenzy, as competing newspapers somehow got hold of the secret Whitehall and Westminster minutes and correspondence which underpinned the defence case. There are, of course, some journalists who will get excited when handed a copy of *Pets' World* if the magic phrase 'Most Secret' has been stamped over the cover of a special issue on poodle hairdos. But the body of documentation released thanks to the Matrix Churchill case provided a unique opportunity. The documents had been weeded so that, for example, the letters and minutes from Number 10, when Margaret Thatcher was prime minister, had been obviously removed from the sequence of correspondence. But, even so, the documents told an astonishing story of how government ministers had evidence dating from 1987 that Matrix

Churchill had been exporting its machine tools to Iraqi munitions factories. The documents expressed Whitehall's concern that the British-made machine tools could well be used in Saddam's programme to acquire weapons of mass destruction: the unholy NBC trinity of nuclear, biological and chemical warfare. The documents revealed consistent and well-founded worries that the machine tools could also assist in Saddam's missile and supergun programmes, created to deliver the NBC weapons to Iraq's enemies. Despite all these concerns, the government's approval for the shipments of Matrix Churchill technology continued, up to twenty-four hours before the invasion of Kuwait.

That ministers – lots of ministers – knew all along put the Customs and Excise prosecution of the Matrix Churchill Three in a lurid light. It appeared, on the face of the evidence, that Abraham, Allen and Henderson had been unfairly prosecuted for what was common knowledge in the corridors of power. Worse, the twist emerged during the trial that Henderson had been an effective and highly valued agent for the British Secret Intelligence Service, MI6, and was one of the sources for that knowledge. It now appeared that not just ordinary British businessmen but a real-life James Bond had been prosecuted. Henderson told Thames Television's *This Week*, transmitted on 19 November 1992, after the not-guilty verdict: 'If the Iraqis had found that I had provided information to British intelligence, yes, I could have ended up in an Iraqi jail. But I never expected I would end up in a British jail.'

Worst of all, four ministers, three of whom were in the Cabinet, had signed public interest immunity certificates, asserting that all the documents should stay secret because their disclosure would endanger the national interest. It was further argued that they were not relevant to the case. But Judge Brian Smedley agreed that a good part of the documents be released to the defence. They proved to be highly relevant and endangered not the national interest but ministerial reputations. The attorney general's argument that the ministers were under a duty to sign the gagging certificates did not cut much ice. The obvious deduction was that if the judge had been more supine to those in power three patriots could have gone to prison. The cover-up lay exposed.

The air was thick with conspiracy. The shadow of Dr Gerald Bull, a real-life Dr Strangelove assassinated in 1990 in Belgium by unknown hand, wandered again across the national stage, mystifying newspaper readers with the extraordinary story of the supergun. Photographs of the supergun, its tubing built in Sheffield, reappeared in the newspapers, renewing the controversy of whether it could ever have worked. The Israeli secret service, MOSSAD, raced across the stage after the shade of Dr Bull. A Chilean arms dealer, Carlos R. Cardoen, took a bow, as did the branch manager of an Italian bank in Atlanta, Georgia, through which flowed billions of Iraqi money for arms. Serving Cabinet ministers who had authorized the arming of Iraq or had been on selling trips to Baghdad tiptoed from the spotlight.

In the thrill of the chase, many reporters got lost in thickets of arcane and impenetrable detail, concentrating on rehashing supergun or luxuriating in the fine detail of the Matrix Churchill shipments to the exclusion of a great deal else. In particular, the question as to which of our political leaders was responsible for the circumstances in which British troops, come the Gulf War, had to stare down British-made muzzles remained unanswered. The hunt lost much of its edge when prime minister John Major announced that the respected judge Lord Justice Scott would hold a judicial inquiry into whether ministers had misled the House of Commons or broken government guidelines concerning the arms trade with Iraq. This move also usefully provided ministers and others with a copper-bottomed excuse not to provide answers to pertinent questions. The line 'We're waiting for Scott' was uttered by ministers with the same vacant intensity as that of the tramp Vladimir, in Samuel Beckett's avant-garde play, 'We're waiting for Godot.' Fleet Street wandered off in search of softer and more entertaining stories. Windsor Castle went up in smoke. The chancellor of the exchequer was falsely accused of buying a bottle of 'recession-busting champagne' and a packet of twenty Raffles cigarettes from a Threshers off-licence in an area of Paddington frequented by the *demi-monde*. Iraqgate – an irritating yet concise coinage – gave way to what could only be called 'Threshergate'.

The Economist explained the waning interest in Iraqgate: 'any issue to which the Insight investigative team of the *Sunday Times* rightly devotes four pages will not cause serious difficulties to a government. The detail is too complicated, the essence too elusive.' Thus Fleet Street's attitude towards Iraqgate went from mega-scandal to complete yawn in about ten days. Such ennui may be of relief to the 'great and the good' who knew of the secret trade or took part in the cover-up, but it is a disservice to those who expect better from our government than a programme of 'refined truth', tempered by incompetence.

The story of how Britain armed Iraq starts more than two and a half thousand years ago in 586 BC with an event marked by contemporary popular music culture in the Boney M hit 'Rivers of Babylon'. This was when King Nebuchadnezzar – who perhaps might be considered the first Nazi – conquered Jerusalem, destroyed the Great Temple and brought thousands of Jews to captivity in Babylon. Psalm 137 recorded the wretchedness of the Jews: 'by the rivers of Babylon, there we sat down, yea, we wept, when we remembered Zion.' The destruction of the Jewish temple marked the apogee of Babylon's power, but nemesis was at hand. The king of Persia, Cyrus the Great, invaded what is now modern Iraq, crushed the Babylonians and released the Jews. Strange to think that two and a half millennia on the same alliances and enmities, however tacit and uncomfortable, dominate the grand strategy of the Middle East.

The glory of Nebuchadnezzar's forty-three-year reign has long obsessed Saddam. In 1979, when he stepped up to take formal command of Iraq, having been its effective ruler for a decade, he said: 'Nebuchadnezzar stirs in me everything relating to pre-Islamic ancient history. I am reminded that any human being with broad horizons, faith and feeling can act wisely but practically, attain his goals and become a great man who makes his country into a great state. And what is most important to me about Nebuchadnezzar is the link between the Arabs' abilities and the liberation of Palestine. Nebuchadnezzar was, after all, an Arab from Iraq, albeit ancient Iraq. Nebuchadnezzar was the one who brought the Jewish slaves from Palestine. That is why I like to remind the Arabs, Iraqis in particular, of their historical responsibilities. It is a burden that should not stop them from action, but rather spur them into action because of their history.'

This speech gives a number of insights to Saddam. First, obviously, he sees himself as a strong man in the grip of destiny, following in the steps of Nebuchadnezzar, but his phrasing echoes more recent examples of the superhero in Mussolini and Hitler. Second, Saddam is a man of intelligence and some sensitivity to the nuances of language and expression. Almost certainly someone else wrote that speech, but you have to have an ear for words to select a competent speech-writer. Contrast Saddam's level of eloquence with, say, Idi Amin, the tyrant of Uganda, or Nicolae Ceausescu, the strong man of Romania. Amin's grip on English idiom was so idiosyncratic that it became a column in *Punch* magazine; the Genius of the Carpathians barked a jumbled Marxist-Leninist patois, slurred by his speech defect. So Saddam is not a savage, nor patently mad, but a comparative sophisticate. Third, he wants action, he wants to be strong, he wants the force to express his will. Fourth, he hates Jews.

Comparing a dictatorship with Nazi Germany is too pat, too easily done. The horrors of the Nazi Holocaust were on such a scale and carried out by such a well-constructed civilization that they should not be lightly or inaccurately invoked. But from boyhood Saddam fell under the influence of a guardian of the Nazi flame. Saddam's favourite Nazi uncle was Khairallah Tulfah, who was also his foster-father and father-in-law, and later became the governor of Baghdad. Saddam was growing up during the Second World War with Tulfah, and his young nephew, very much on the side of the Nazis and their Arab allies who tried (and failed) to expel the British imperialists from the Iraqi homeland. Patriotic sentiment may have pushed some Iraqis in favour of the Axis powers, but Tulfah was a true believer. Some idea of just how Nazi his thinking was can be gleaned from a pamphlet he wrote, published and widely circulated in Iraq by the national publishing house in 1981: 'Three Whom God Should Not Have Created: Persians, Jews and Flies.' Persians, Tulfah wrote, are 'animals God created in the shape of humans'. Jews are a 'mixture of the dirt and leftovers of diverse peoples'. But with flies Tulfah's hateful imagination let him down. Flies are a trifling creation 'whom we do not understand God's purpose in creating'. This was the intellectual environment in which the boy Saddam grew up.

Saddam Hussein was born on 28 April 1937 in a dusty village on the banks of the Tigris 100 miles north of Baghdad, not far from the provincial town of Tikrit. Little is known about his natural father, but his step-father, Ibrahim al-Hassan, was a brute who beat the small boy. To protect himself Saddam carried around a steel bar. At the age of ten his foster-father, Tulfah, is said to have given him the present of his dreams: a revolver.

The rumours in the Iraqi exile community – a not necessarily reliable source of information – say that before Saddam was out of his teens he had committed murder. He went to Baghdad in his late teens, and joined the Baathist Party at the age of twenty in 1957. In essence, the Baathists are an Arab reworking of the Nazis. Instead of domination of Europe by the Aryan race, the Baathists look towards a pan-Arab state, but the tunes seem startlingly familiar. In the late fifties Baghdad resembled twenties Berlin, with Iraqi Communists and Baathists (taking the part of the Brown Shirts) fighting bloody street battles for dominance. In this blood-spilling, Saddam began to make a name for himself. His moment came in 1959, the year after the British-backed Hashemite monarchy had been ousted by a temporary alliance of the two factions. Displaced from power by the Communists, the Baathists decided to assassinate Iraq's president, Brigadier Abdel-Karim Qassem. They bungled it, shooting Qassem's driver, but only wounding the president. In the shoot-out, Saddam himself was wounded. In the official hagiographies he had had to extract a bullet from his own leg because no doctor could be found. True: the Baathist sympathizer who arrived, now Dr Tahsin Moallah, was at that time a medical student.

The wound, the doctor said years later, was superficial, 'like a knife wound'. Nevertheless, young Saddam had been blooded in the cause.

The Baathists seized power in 1963, but botched the fine details of terror, and were themselves ousted by the army later that year. During the next few years Saddam led a low-profile existence in exile, a Baathist hood, knocking around the coffee shops of Egypt. The summer of 1968 was the apogee of flower power, peace and love. It found Saddam – no hippie, he – riding on a tank, crashing through the gates of the presidential palace to launch the second and this time lasting Baathist coup. He was rewarded with being the power behind the throne, deputy to President Ahmed Hassan al-Bakr. Once Saddam was in place, the blood began to flow.

No one in the West, least of all ministers in the British government, should have been in any doubt as to the true nature of the Baathist regime in Iraq from 1968 onwards. The room in which I am writing is cluttered with report after report after report, freely available from the early seventies onwards, which provided, in stomach-churning detail, the evidence of torture, hanging, execution and systematic terror that ruled and continues to rule Iraq. It was – is – a secret police state sitting on the world's second biggest oil reserves, malevolence armed with the riches of Croesus. Of all the documents recording Baathist state terror, from the United Nations, Amnesty International, newspaper and television journalists, the volumes of terrified Iraqi exiles, one stands out alone. It was an exhibit in the Matrix Churchill case, raised when Paul Henderson's artful silk, Geoffrey Robertson, was cross-examining his client's MI6 controller, styled Officer A, but identified in court by his cover name John Balson, and, variously, Balscomb and Balstring. No one knows his fifth, real name. The drama of the cross-examination was heightened by Balson being completely hidden from press and public by screens. Such was the mania for secrecy that the cracks between the screens had been covered over with brown paper.

ROBERTSON: And you remember giving him this book which is called *Republic of Fear*?

BALSON: Yes.

ROBERTSON: Which was a book that had been published in 1989. And inviting him to read to understand just how dangerous the characters and personalities he was dealing with were?

BALSON: Yes, and also because I think that is a superb description of the appalling regime in Iraq.

ROBERTSON: I will not quote from it but you accept that its message is, there has been a ruthless and relentless build-up in Iraq of terror?

BALSON: Yes, I agree.

ROBERTSON: And it describes Saddam Hussein as the only genuinely free man in Iraq, as a megalomaniac whose secret police system and courts system had been devised to torture and execute those who were disloyal to the state?

BALSON: Yes.

Republic of Fear (London: Hutchinson, 1989) by Samir al-Khalil would have been a chilling read for Henderson, not quite a conventional history of Saddam's rule but an enquiry into its meaning. The book takes the reader through the early years of Baathist power in great detail with a quiet, discriminating intelligence. The style is unhysterical and as well researched as possible, given the difficulties of establishing facts rather than rumour when ordinary people are afraid to think aloud in front of their own children. According to *Republic of Fear* the Jews of Baghdad were among the first to suffer. The Baathists arrested seventeen spies in late 1968 – of whom thirteen were Jews – and after a risible show trial in early 1969 hanged them to public delirium. In that year public executions became a regular fixture on the calendar, taking place on 20 February, 14 and 30 April, 15 May, 21 and 25 August, 8 September, and 26 November. As the Jewish community either were executed or fled, the Baathist meat-grinder consumed anyone who took its fancy: Arabs,

Christians, Kurds, the Sunni, the Shia. (Islam is divided into two branches: Sunni and Shia. Although the majority of Iraqis are Shia, like the Iranians, Saddam and his henchmen are Sunni, in common with most of the Arab world.) Being a loyal Baathist was no guarantee of safety, for Saddam's rule required a conveyor-belt of 'spies' and 'traitors' to admit their crimes to feed his paranoia. The closer you were to Saddam, the higher the stakes. Iraq was sucked into a vortex of violence from which it has yet to escape.

Reading the details of horror at first numbs; then, the mind, incapable of taking it all in, starts to switch off. That sounds uncaring and more than a little cynical. Here, then, is a test for the reader. Take the Amnesty International report on torture in Iraq, published in 1985, which lists thirty different varieties. Can you read all thirty without losing concentration, without wanting to think of something, anything else?

(1) Beatings on all parts of the body, particularly the head, genitals, and spine, involving slapping, kicking or punching. Blows are reportedly administered with fists, feet, rubber truncheons (some with a metal rod inside), rope, hose, wooden sticks or whips.

(2) Falaqa: beating the soles of the feet while the victim is strapped to a table with the legs raised. Sometimes the victim is then said to be forced to walk or run around the room on hot salty water.

(3) Al-Mangana: clamp-like instrument which is placed over the toes and tightened.

(4) Extracting finger and toe nails.

(5) Applying pressure to the eyes through blindfolds.

(6) Suspending the victim by handcuffed wrists from the wall, ceiling or a ladder for several hours.

(7) Suspending the victim by the wrists or ankles from a rotating fan in the ceiling, and beating him/her as he/she rotates.

(8) Forcing the victim to stand on one leg and/or to keep the arms raised for long periods, accompanied by beating if the position is not maintained.

(9) Applying electricity to sensitive parts of the body, includ-

ing the nostrils, ears, temples, nipples, kidney region, fingers, toes and genitals. This is said to be administered with a truncheon-like instrument with a cable attached to one end (known as the 'electric stick' [this sounds like an electric cattle prod]) or with electrodes.

(10) Forcing the victim to step in a bath full of water through which an electric current is running.

(11) Burning parts of the body with cigarettes, hot domestic irons, electric hotplates or gas flames.

(12) 'Electric chair': a metal plaque fixed to the wall comprising five bars which lacerate the back of the victim who is tied to it.

(13) Tying the victim by the wrists and ankles to a cross-bar which is then turned over flames (like a roasting spit).

(14) Fixing the head of the victim in a cabin with intense ultra-violet rays, which burn the eyes.

(15) Placing the half-naked victim in a heated closet full of steam, then reducing the temperature drastically.

(16) Pouring cold water on to the victim while in the open air in near-freezing temperatures.

(17) Pouring water over the nose and mouth of the victim, causing near suffocation.

(18) Throwing the victim to a distance of 2 to 3 metres from a type of ejector chair.

(19) 'The wheel': a machine to which the victim is tied and then stretched by turning a handle.

(20) Sexual abuse or assaults, including forcing the victim to sit on bottle necks or inserting a bottle or wire into the rectum.

(21) Prolonged solitary confinement.

(22) Mutilation of the body, including gouging out the eyes, cutting off the nose, ears, breasts, penis, axing the limbs, peeling the skin or cutting it open with a sharp instrument, hammering nails into the body; threats of such mutilation.

(23) Threatening the victim with the arrest, torture and rape of relatives.

(24) Forcing the victim to listen to or watch other detainees being tortured.

(25) Playing during interrogation or in the cell tape recordings of animal noises or of family members crying or being insulted.

(26) Threatening the victim with death or execution, or with being charged with a capital offence.

(27) Subjecting the victim to mock executions, including by shooting, strangulation and drowning.

(28) Degrading the victim by using obscene language or insults or by forcing him/her to undress in front of guards of the opposite sex.

(29) Deprivation of sleep, food, water, fresh air, toilet or washing facilities, visits by relatives, and medical treatment.

(30) Offering the victims 'rewards' in exchange for an undertaking to remain politically unaffiliated.

Those bored with the recitation of tortures and horrors of the Baathist regime may care to study the really novel cruelties. Three examples suffice. First, *Republic of Fear* cites the 1974 arrest of the Masonic plotters; the average age of those rounded up must have been in their seventies. The arrests were sparked by the discovery in a safe deposit box, opened by the authorities after the expiry of a fifteen-year limit, of an invitation list to a party that had taken place in 1942 at the house of Major Chadwick who had left Iraq in 1958. The oldest victim (ninety-two) and prime culprit had joined a Masonic Lodge in Bombay in 1908, a full decade before the collapse of the Ottoman Empire. Al-Khalil comments: 'Imputing insidious links to a foreign power had obviously degenerated into pure farce.'

Second, John Bulloch and Harvey Morris in *Saddam's War* (London: Faber, 1991), describe an incident in early 1973, when two men were being tortured by one of the Baathist psychopaths, Nadhim Kzar, in charge of the new department of internal state security. The witness who did not confess under duress lived to tell this tale. He was described by another Iraqi to the authors: 'This is a man of great integrity, very meticulous. But he still has nightmares about what he saw . . . [A third man] came into the room, picked up Dukhail [the victim] and dropped him into a bath of acid. And then he watched while the body dissolved.'

The witness recognized the third man. He was the vice-president of Iraq at the time, after all.

Third, after Saddam took over from al-Bakr in 1979 he did not change his approach even to the most courteously expressed dissent. In March 1982 his invasion of Iran two years before was looking increasingly reckless. Far from collapsing under the strains of the overthrow of the Shah and the Revolutionary Terror, the Iranian army had proved tougher than the Iraqis expected. After the Iranians overran Iraqi positions in Khorram-shahr, Saddam called a Cabinet meeting when he innocently enquired whether anyone thought it would be a good idea for him to go. The health minister, Riyadh Ibrahim, unwisely suggested that Saddam might step down for a few months. The two men stepped outside for a quiet discussion. The remaining Cabinet ministers heard a shot, then silence. Saddam returned to move on to the next business.

The 1980–88 war with Iran was a feast of blood. It was to claim a million casualties, dead and wounded. Saddam started it. When it looked as though he was going to lose, he broke the rules.

> If in some smothering dreams you too could pace
> Behind the wagon that we flung him in,
> And watch the white eyes writhing in his face,
> His hanging face, like a devil's sick of sin;
> If you could hear, at every jolt, the blood
> Come gargling from the froth-corrupted lungs,
> Obscene as cancer, bitter as the cud
> Of vile, incurable sores on innocent tongues . . .

Although the war poet Wilfred Owen was killed in the week before the Armistice, in poems like 'Dulce et Decorum Est' he did humanity a lasting service by crystallizing the common soldiers' revulsion at chemical warfare. At the end of the 1914–18 war, the international community sought to ban chemical weapons for all time. This led to the world-wide ban, drawn up in the Geneva Accord of 1925. The protocol followed two previous agreements, the first, signed at St Petersburg in 1868, called on nations to forswear the use of projectiles 'charged with fulminating or inflammable substances'; the second, the Hague Convention of 1889, urged states to 'abstain from the use of projectiles, the object of which is the diffusion of asphyxiating or deleterious gases'. The Geneva Accord stated grandly: 'The use in war of asphyxiating, poisonous or other gases, and of all analogous liquids, materials or devices, has been justly condemned by the general opinion of the civilized world' and called on signatories to prohibit their use. Iraq signed the Accord in 1931.

Remarkably, ordinary people's disgust at chemical weapons was shared by their leaders. Adolf Hitler feared to use the nerve gas tabun, invented by his Nazi scientists, because he thought, wrongly, that the Allies had stocks too. But another factor which stayed his hand from using gas against Allied troops – as opposed to against the helpless victims in the death camp gas chambers – was that he had suffered exposure to mustard gas and was blinded for a time in the final stages of the First World War. He wrote: 'My eyes had turned into glowing coals; it had grown dark around me.'

Saddam had no such compunction. When the Iranian human wave offensives looked like breaching Iraqi lines in late 1983 and early 1984 during the Iran-Iraq war, Saddam broke the Accord.

The Iraqis denied the Iranian claims, but the United Nations sent four medical and chemical experts to Iran to establish the facts in March 1984. The UN experts published a report on their findings on 26 March 1984, which was and is freely available from the UN. It, like many other documents on the reality of the Baathist regime, makes for queasy reading. The UN found incontrovertible evidence that the Iraqis had used mustard gas 'the King of gases' and the chemical nerve agent tabun when they bombed unprotected Iranian troops who had launched an offensive against the Majnoon islands, a strategic battleground north of the southern Iraqi city of Basra.

Tabun, first developed by the Nazis, is lethal but quickly disperses. Mustard gas is not so much a killer as a disabler, the damage it does to the human body causing immense loss of morale to troops. The UN scientists found the chemical weapons changed skin colour to red, to wine and in some cases to black. The areas most affected were found to be

> the armpits, scrotum and penis, followed by the groin and the inner surface of the elbows and knees, possibly because of the greater sensitivity of the skin ... Very dark lesions had appeared on the genitals.
>
> Subsequently, blisters filled with a yellowish fluid, under pressure, had appeared, assuming a domed shape. They ranged from a few millimetres to several decimetres in size, in some cases reaching enormous proportions.

(A decimetre is a tenth of a metre, roughly three and a half inches long.) Other symptoms included massive loss of white-blood cells, nausea, vomiting, incontinence, limb tremors.

In late March 1984 Dr Alastair Hay, a reader in chemical pathology at Leeds University, followed in the footsteps of the UN team. He has made his personal notes, taken while interviewing the chemical weapon victims, available to me. They are sparsely written but tell the story well enough:

> Hassani Abedideh, age 19. Three weeks ago. Eyes OK now, was worse before. Blisters everywhere, even on head. Like grain chemicals – like ammonia. Up to 12 planes. Low when dropped. Not much noise. Exploded hitting ground yellow smoke and liquid. Burnt a bit immediately. Fighters came – dropped more. After an hour felt sick.

> Hamid Rezaee. Burned face – eyes bloodshot – watering. Nose and mouth encrusted. In Iraq – near Basra. Five soldiers (Jofeira area). Long range artillery. 2.30 a.m. Had hacking cough. Nose and mouth congested – phlegm. After explosion – smoke had sulphurous smell. One shell cut colleague's leg. Didn't feel anything immediately ... After few hours felt sick – taken to hospital. Before washed, eyes were burning. After

showering skin still burning. Large burn on left arm – was first blister. Small blisters on right arm at elbows. Still blisters between legs – large burns. Still peeling off scrotum – clearly very painful.

There is more, too terrible to rehearse here.

It was Saddam's use of chemical weapons (and also the Iranians' use of pitifully ill-prepared teenage 'Basij' warriors in the human wave offensives) which caused the then British foreign secretary, Sir Geoffrey Howe, to draw up a set of guidelines so that British firms would not profit from or prolong the slaughter. The precise wording is important to the story, as the guidelines were dipped in a series of Whitehall acid-baths until they were bleached of all meaning. Howe told the House of Commons on 29 October 1985:

> The United Kingdom has been strictly impartial in the conflict between Iran and Iraq and has refused to allow the supply of lethal defence equipment to either side. In order to reinforce our policy of doing everything possible to see this tragic conflict brought to the earliest possible end, we decided in December 1984 to apply thereafter the following set of guidelines to all deliveries of defence equipment to Iran and Iraq:
>
> (i) We should maintain our consistent refusal to supply any lethal equipment to either side.
>
> (ii) Subject to that overriding consideration, we should attempt to fulfil existing contracts and obligations.
>
> (iii) We should not, in future, approve orders for any defence equipment which, in our view, would significantly enhance the capability of either side to prolong or exacerbate the conflict.
>
> (iv) In line with this policy, we should continue to scrutinize rigorously all applications for export licences for the supply of defence equipment to Iran and Iraq.

The Howe guidelines were an expression of piety, a stake in the moral high ground belied by the evidence. Close textual analysis reveals that there was a great deal of ambiguity and room for interpretation within the guidelines. From 1980 to 1990 Britain exported a treasure trove of defence equipment for Saddam's war machine, including known and easily identifiable raw ingredients for chemical weapons, sodium cyanide and sodium sulphide in the late eighties. Other goodies Baghdad-bound included plutonium, zirconium, thorium oxide, gas spectrometers, all essential for nuclear technology; explosives; electronic surveillance equipment, including advanced cipher and decoding equipment, radio frequency hoppers, burst trasmitters and a long range radio system; pistols, rifles and shotguns, artillery fire control and fast assault craft and night vision equipment. Not forgetting the Matrix Churchill machine tools, which ended up in Saddam's weapons factories. The Matrix Churchill shipments did not represent a strange aberration, but were par for the course.

The DTI had originally informed the House of Commons Trade and Industry Select Committee in July 1991 that Britain had also exported two shipments of thiodiglycol and thiodyl chloride, both raw ingredients or precursors for mustard gas. Following an uproar from the opposition, the DTI went back to their books and discovered those two chemicals had not been exported to Iraq. Rather, they were on the list as examples of the type of chemical which should not be exported to countries like Iraq. When the row started, the then trade secretary Peter Lilley condemned his shadow, Gordon Brown, for stirring up a 'silly season story'. Prime minister John Major explained in a letter, published on 1 August 1991, to Gordon Brown that many of the goods 'were exported in minute quantities or for clearly harmless use, and all applications for export licences . . . were carefully vetted by the inter-departmental group which was staffed by experts whose integrity and professionalism you have impugned'. On 8 August 1991, the *Daily Telegraph* reported an apology by the DTI's press office, Andrew Marre: 'I can only put it down to a breakdown in communications.'

After the DTI's cock-up was revealed it emerged in 1991 that the records for chemical exports to Iraq were not kept beyond a couple of years. Despite the Howe guidelines, despite Britain's world lead in the fight to ban all chemical weapons, no one in Whitehall could say for certain whether we had helped Saddam to make mustard gas and nerve gas. Dr Hay drily noted in a letter to the Trade and Industry Select Committee: 'It would have been reassuring to know that Britain did not contribute in any way to the development of Iraq's chemical warfare programme. It now looks as though we will never know what was sent.'

If incompetence was one signal quality of Britain's trade with Saddam, then 'refined truth' was another. We did less business with Saddam than the French, the Germans – who supplied the bulk of the Iraqis' chemical warfare technology – and the Soviet Union, who competed to be his principal arms suppliers in the seventies and eighties. But this was more an accident of history than policy based upon distaste at Saddam's inhumanity. After the fall in 1979 of our main customer in the Middle East, the Shah of Iran, UK Ltd fell over itself to became Saddam's sweetheart.

There was a little local difficulty in that at the time of the Shah's fall relations between Britain and Iraq were frosty, because Saddam's military intelligence arm, the Estikhbarat, had assassinated a former Iraqi prime minister, Abdul Razzaq al-Nayef, on the streets of London in July 1978. Following the murder, Britain expelled some eleven Iraqi diplomats; Iraq retaliated by placing a trade embargo on British goods. But the cadavers of Saddam's victims did not seem to stand in the way of Anglo-Iraq trade for long, as we shall see. On 5 July 1979, British foreign secretary Lord Carrington was welcomed to Baghdad and Iraq announced that it would lift its trade embargo against the UK. The foreign secretary heralded a 'new page in UK/Iraq relations' and declared that Britain wished to boost trade between the two new friends. Hot on Lord Carrington's heels in October came the then trade minister Cecil Parkinson and a month later, the then secretary of state for trade and industry, John Nott. The flow of ministerial visits did not cease throughout the war years.

From long before the Howe guidelines formalized Britain's policy of even-handedness, we were giving a secret helping hand to Saddam. Throughout the bloody war with Iran, the longest conventional struggle between two states this century, Britain sided with Iraq.

Consider the conflicting evidence. The public policy was first stated in Sir Geoffrey Howe's preamble to the 1985 guidelines: 'The United Kingdom has been strictly impartial in the conflict between Iran and Iraq.' This line was repeated by different ministers throughout the war years, and emphasized when ministers faced difficulties because of public revulsion at Saddam's chemical weapon attacks. The secret policy was somewhat different, hiding behind the reluctance of Whitehall and Westminster to disclose information.

Study the trade credits awarded by the British Government to Iraq. Trade credits, approved through the Export Credits Guarantee Department, are the mechanism by which the British govenment 'insures' British firms against bad debts when they export to foreign countries. If the country does not pay up, the taxpayer makes good the company's loss. In the five years from 1980 to 1985, when Sir Geoffrey announced Britain's impartiality between Iran and Iraq, the government provided Saddam with £2388 million in credits; for the years 1980 to 1990 the figure rises to £3517 million.

Thanks to Whitehall's enthusiasm for Saddam, at the time of the invasion of Kuwait he had been forwarded medium term export credits worth £1140 million alone, though the Iraqis had not taken up £265 million of that largess. All figures are from the Export Credits Guarantee Department (ECGD) evidence to the Trade and Industry Select Committee, November 1991. Of the £3.5 billion staked on Saddam over the decade – a massive running bet – we lost something close to a billion when Saddam invaded Kuwait and refused to repay his debts. The first figure which emerged in the summer of 1990 was a billion, which was subsequently reduced to an estimated £940 million when the DTI gave evidence to the 1991 Select Committee. The figure has not yet been finalized, but the ECGD warned the Select Committee: 'At this stage it is difficult to forecast to what extent claims payments will be recovered, and what therefore the eventual net loss might be. It would be prudent, however, to assume that recovery will be a difficult and extended process.'

As the practice on ECGD lines was for ministers not to disclose the figures, the extent of British exposure to Saddam was only revealed in 1991 – long after Sir Geoffrey's 1985 statement to the Commons that Britain was even-handed in the war between Iran and Iraq. (Britain's export credit exposure to Iran was on a much smaller scale. According to the ECGD no medium-term trade credits were issued in the 1980s.) The secrecy helped the government conceal the full truth from the taxpayer. Iraq did well out of the ECGD, Britain less so, losing an amount just short of a billion pounds – money, some might say, which might have been spent on more deserving causes than Saddam's bulging war chest.

The second piece of evidence is the list of visits British trade ministers made to Iraq. (This clearly does not include all visits by ministers to Baghdad, some of whom were anxious to keep their time spent supping with the Iraqis as little noticed as possible, as we shall see.) From 1981 onwards British trade ministers went on yearly pilgrimages to Baghdad, or invited their Iraqi opposite numbers to London, as part of the United Kingdom/Iraq Joint Commissions on Economic and Technical Co-operation.

John Biffen, Margaret Thatcher's whimsical and entertaining waspish secretary of state for trade, went to Baghdad from 30 September to 5 October 1981. In 1983 trade minister Paul Channon received an Iraqi delegation, led by trade minister Hassan Ali Saleh, in London from 3 to 7 October 1983. Channon expanded British trade credits from cash and short credit lines to medium term projects and a £250-million loan. Although this money could not be spent on lethal weapons, it served to release civilian funds to Iraq's war effort. Later that year and in 1984 Saddam repeatedly used mustard and nerve gas against the Iranians, to horrific effect. The breaking of the Geneva Accord had no impact on the trade missions: Channon returned to Baghdad, from 3 to 6 November 1984. Channon and Hassan Ali were in London in 1985, meeting from 25 to 28 November, the last meeting. That year Marconi (UK) won a contract for Iraqi army microwave transmitters; RACAL was allowed to sell to Iraq an advanced frequency military radio; and also sold to Iraq were 300 British military vehicles. In 1986 Channon, an Establishment oyster, was replaced as trade minister by a piece of Establishment true grit, Alan Clark. He met Hassan Ali in Baghdad from 8 to 10 November 1986. In 1987, Clark hosted the Commission on 23 and 24 September in London, meeting with a new face, Mohammed Mehdi Saleh. In 1988 Tony Newton, the chancellor of the Duchy of Lancaster and trade minister went to Baghdad from 5 November to 7 November. In 1989 Lord Trefgarne, the new trade minister, hosted Mohammed Mehdi Saleh in London from 27 November to 30 November. With the exception of 1982 Britain never missed a year. In the same period there were no ministerial visits to Iran. (By a strange quirk of luck I witnessed the first British ministerial visit to Iran for thirteen years, when Lady Chalker choppered down to give succour to the dying Kurds in the spring of 1991.)

Whitehall knew Saddam to be a tyrant, but he was our tyrant. In British, European and American eyes Saddam was standing up to the fundamentalist mullahs of revolutionary Islam, who had overthrown the West's good friend, the Shah, and threatened to export the revolution to the reactionary but pro-Western oil monarchies of the Gulf. Revolutionary Iran was the true enemy. Saddam was, in the terms of the *realpolitik* which ruled the West during the Reagan–Thatcher years, our enemy's enemy, and, therefore, our friend. No one thought through the possibility that sometimes, in the words of Valentin Ceausescu, the eldest son of the late Romanian dictator: 'Our enemy's enemy can also be our enemy.'

In the decade in which Saddam refined state terror to the nth degree, invaded a neighbouring nation state and broke the Geneva Accord against chemical weapons, our ministers rewarded his malevolence with close to £1 billion worth of goods on the never-never. He has yet to pay up.

Tortuous policy and tortured truth. The two defining features of Britain's trade with Iraq twist and turn in the wind, like twin villains on a gibbet.

CHAPTER
TWO

The training programme was the responsibility of a tough, no-
nonsense officer named John Cuckney . . . He was altogether
different from the average MI5 officer. He refused to submit to
the monotony of the dark pinstripe, preferring bolder styles . . .
Cuckney described various situations, such as entering prem-
ises without a warrant, or invading an individual's privacy,
where the dilemma might arise. He made it clear that MI5
operated on the basis of the Eleventh Commandment – 'Thou
shalt not get caught' – and that in the event of apprehension
there was very little that the office could do to protect its staff.

Thus wrote former and embittered British spy Peter Wright in
his autobiography *Spycatcher: The Candid Autobiography of a Senior
Intelligence Officer* (New York: Viking, 1987).

In all the muddle and murk over the story of Matrix
Churchill, it seems to have been forgotten that a key figure in the
sale of Britain's biggest machine tool company to the Iraqis in
October 1987 was the same man who instructed Spycatcher Peter
Wright 'Thou shalt not get caught' when he joined spy school.
Sir John Cuckney is one of the most powerful and influential
figures in the City of London, such a model of probity that he
was asked by the government to set up a trust for the victims of
the late Robert Maxwell's pensions swindle. Sir John does indeed
cut a debonair dash, and enjoys throwing a few toffees at the
newspapermen and women. He has told journalists that his

hobbies include dipping his worry beads into cool water as well as 'medieval embroidery and yak stalking'. Thanks to *Spycatcher*, we now know that he was also what Fleet Street likes to call a Class One, Grade A spook. Of course, there is no precise mention of Sir John's espionage activities in his lengthy curriculum vitae in *Who's Who*, but an interesting line: 'attachment to War Office (Civil Asst, Gen. Staff, until 1957)', which clearly covers a multitude of possibilities.

It would be surprising if he doesn't keep in touch with the old office from time to time. Would it have been surprising if the sale of the company by the TI group to the Iraqis had not come to the attention of the British government? Sir John was deputy chairman.

In 1987 the company which was to become Matrix Churchill was in dire financial trouble with a diminishing order book. Then named TI Machine Tools, it had been established in the late sixties through the merger of Charles Churchill Limited and Coventry Gauge and Tool Limited. In 1983 TI Machine Tools Limited had bought up Alfred Herbert Limited from the receivers. But years of trading and manufacturing skills looked like being lost for good in the late eighties. Company director Paul Henderson, who had made his way up from the shop-floor, had knocked on a lot of doors in the City, but had failed to get the finance needed for a management buy-out. Closure loomed.

Clippety-clop, clippety-clop: the somewhat off-white knight from Baghdad, Saddam Hussein, rode to the rescue. Set against Iraq's record on human rights, the government's public utterances of strict impartiality in the Iran-Iraq war and its ban on defence exports which would worsen the conflict, the sale of Matrix Churchill to the Iraqis would appear to conflict with British government policy. But in the context of actual British policy towards Iraq – regular trade visits oiled by billions of pounds' worth of credit for Saddam – the sale falls snugly into place.

The man who effectively bought Matrix Churchill and became a key director was Dr Safa Jawad Habobi, who was one of Saddam's top arms buyers. Habobi was the head of the Nassir

State Enterprise for Mechanical Engineering, but much more important he was a big player in Iraq's nuclear, chemical warfare and conventional arms procurement network, based first at offices off Oxford Street, then in Chiswick, West London. If one goes into a brain-numbing maze of alphabet soup front companies and part-contracts, following British goods through the Chilean weapons firm Cardoen, one ends up back in Baghdad. The maze was not an accident, but a cunning security precaution by Habobi to prevent Western intelligence agencies and Western governments from discovering just how advanced and ambitious Saddam's plans for his war machine were, until too late. A maze of company names is a standard trick for those who have something to hide. Its finest exponent in recent years is the late and partially lamented Robert Maxwell, but that is another story.

Habobi and another player in the Iraqi arms procurement racket, Dr Fadel Kadhum, both worked for Brigadier Hussein Kamil Hassan al-Majid, Saddam's favourite son-in-law. Hussein Kamil is a versatile fellow who, as head of Iraq's Ministry for Industry and Military Industrialization (MIMI), met British MPs and trade ministers like Tony Newton in 1988, but was also in charge of the Al Amn Al Khas, the Special Security Agency. This was set up by Saddam to procure Iraq's superweapons, such as a nuclear bomb, but also to spy on his other myriad of spy networks.

The multitude of names pullulate and confuse. This was deliberate. Matrix Churchill sounds as English as roast beef and poll tax, but it was ultimately owned by the al-Arabi Trading Company, Baghdad. Readers might care to play a counter-confusion mind game: every time they read the words Matrix Churchill, think not of England but of a palm tree and a scimitar slashing through the hot desert air. The Ministry of Industry and Military Industrialization was another Baghdad mind-game, because Western businessmen trading with MIMI sometimes preferred to chop off the last three words of the ministry's full title. The Iraqis were adept at disguising what they were up to. According to the American defence journalist Kenneth R.

Timmerman: 'Whenever the military were stymied in procuring high technology in the West, they simply detailed a civilian establishment to fill out the forms.' For a long time, it suited the West to play along.

As well as buying Matrix Churchill, from 1987 onwards Habobi went on a major shopping spree in the world's arms supermarket, snapping up technology for making nuclear bombs, including uranium centrifuges, chemical weapons, long range artillery rockets and not forgetting Dr Gerald Bull's supergun – perhaps the most literal expression of Freudian 'penis envy' ever entertained.

Far from thwarting Habobi's arms-buying plans, there is no evidence that British intelligence tried to stop him from buying Matrix Churchill in 1987. As one sifts and weighs what we know about Sir John Cuckney and the company – which boasted two British intelligence agents, one active and one dormant, on its staff – the suspicion gels that the sale to Habobi may have been a 'sting' operation against the Iraqis.

The first approach came from the Iraqis, Henderson told the *Financial Times* on 10 November 1992, through their go-between in Britain, Roy Ricks. There are three pertinent pieces of information the reader should bear in mind about Ricks: firstly, he is often described in the newspapers as 'Roy Ricks, an Essex businessman'; the second is that he is a 'name known' to British intelligence, as one of the British intelligence officers told the Matrix Churchill trial; the third is that he was the director of an Iraqi front company with an Iraqi businessman called Anees Waadi. Henderson told the *FT*: 'I didn't think he would get any business out of them and thought we were wasting our time.' He was wrong. The company received a £19 million order for computer numerically controlled (or CNC) lathes to be used in the manufacture of 80-mm, 122-mm and 155-mm shells. Other orders had gone to other British machine tool firms, namely BSA Tools, Colchester Lathes and Wickman Bennett. As the orders came out of the blue – in 1986 there were no exports of British machine tools to Iraq – none of the companies realized such orders could be in breach of the Howe guidelines. That problem would come later.

Later that year TI was again contacted by Ricks the Essex businessman, who said he represented Iraqi interests who wanted to buy Matrix Churchill. On the face of it, the deal looked like a good solution to Matrix Churchill's financial problems. Sir John Cuckney later said that there was nothing unusual about selling Matrix Churchill to an Iraqi company. The price had been a good one and TI had wanted to sell it, went Sir John's thinking according to the *FT*. And with that offering, Sir John slips back into the shadows of our narrative.

There was a catch to the Iraqi gift horse, of course. Henderson told the *FT*: 'There is no doubt in my mind that the business was sold to the Iraqis so that we could monitor them.' That would have amounted to Henderson's informed suspicion, were it not for the Customs prosecution of the Matrix Churchill Three. The defence's main argument throughout was that far from keeping the government in the dark, Henderson and another Matrix Churchill executive, Mark Gutteridge, who was never charged, had informed British intelligence of what the Iraqis were up to. To head off that line of defence, the Crown silk, Alan Moses, called two British intelligence officers, first officer B, and known to the court by his cover name, Michael Ford, who was oblique, then Balson, who was more forthright. It was a historic though funny-peculiar occasion because both officers were examined in 'open court'. That is, the jury and the press were not thrown out and the proceedings held in camera, as had been previous practice in trials involving British intelligence officers. Press and members of the public whose identity had been checked were permitted to hear the evidence, but not to see the officers from the dark side of Whitehall. The spies' evidence was given from behind screens with special James Bond-style brown paper wrapping covering the cracks between the screens, lest anyone unauthorized take a peep. Balson looked strange to those who were allowed to see him, wearing what looked like fake glasses and with his hair parted down the middle in the fashion of a socially awkward vicar at an Edwardian tea party. But Fleet Street's finest can be trusted to rise to the challenge. One reporter bent down to sneak a look underneath the screen at the first intelligence officer's shoes. He reported they were brown. Another reporter had a look, and said they were black. Such is the state of open government in our country a few years before the second millennium.

The secret purpose of the British government was spelt out in the Matrix Churchill trial by Henderson's MI6 controller, Balson. Hiding behind his wrapping paper, Balson was almost passionate: 'It is our job to collect strategic intelligence which is vital to threats to Britain. The three things we were most worried about concerning Iraq were nuclear capability, long range missile capability, biological and chemical. These, and trying to find out about efforts to obtain such technology [which] . . . involved these companies in London . . . Conventional weapons were less a strategic intelligence priority because it would obviously be a great threat to stability in the Middle East, even to Europe itself, if Saddam Hussein had developed these weapons of mass destruction. And thank God he didn't, as far as we know.'

Henderson's silk, Geoffrey Robertson, twitted Balson a little more: 'You told him you were not so interested in merely a few contracts for conventional weapons?'

Balson replied: 'In respect of just my service, not in respect of HMG, or for the law or anything like that.'

This, then, is the secret MI6 justification for tearing up the Howe guidelines as far as they covered Matrix Churchill. It was an acceptable lesser evil to arm Saddam with conventional weapons, even those which would prolong the conflict, for the greater good of obtaining intelligence on Saddam's superweapon ambitions. It is a nice argument, even if it makes a monkey out of Sir Geoffrey Howe and his colleagues in government. But Balson's argument is based on an assumption that Britain would get the better of the Faustian Pact. No one, it seems, sat down to consider the question, 'Who gets the fat, who gets the lean?' No one, that is, until that awful morning on 2 August 1990 when

British intelligence woke up to realize that Saddam had the fat and Saddam had the lean.

Although the MI6 man, Balson, was the more expansive and direct of the two intelligence officers, it was the MI5 man, Officer B or Ford, who ran the British intelligence agent inside Matrix Churchill to begin with. It must surely be one of life's happy accidents that before former MI5 officer Sir John Cuckney played his part in selling the firm to the Iraqis, MI5 knew they had an agent inside the company to spy on the new owners.

Whereas Balson almost gushed when giving his evidence, extracting information from Ford was like getting blood out of stone. He did not volunteer anything to Robertson; rather, the barrister might get something if he dropped questions before, behind and around the target. Reading the transcript of Ford's evidence is like watching artillery range-finding. For example, it took the barrister an age to discover who Ford actually worked for, and then by accident. The intelligence, like much else in the whole story, came obliquely. It leaked out while Ford was telling the jury about the sharing of information from Matrix Churchill inside Whitehall: it was early days 'and it was unsure what we were dealing with. Was it a problem of technology transfer, or a matter that should be addressed by my sister company? I think you will probably find that it went to both.'

ROBERTSON: Your sister being Five or Six?
FORD: Six.
ROBERTSON: So you are in Five?
FORD: Correct.

Reporters covering the trial could have been forgiven for thinking that Ford would have done his country proud under torture.

The British intelligence agent inside Matrix Churchill before Henderson was the firm's then marketing manager, Mark Gutteridge. Ford said he first met Gutteridge 'around the Christmas of 1986', that is long before the sale of Matrix Churchill to the Iraqis.

One of the fascinations of the trial was the insight it gave to the strict procedures and odd little idiosyncrasies of the spy business. Contact notes and source reports, 'lurs', 'turs', and methods of procedure were like crumbs dropped from a secret feast. The most interesting of the 500 or so Matrix Churchill documents which littered what used to be called Fleet Street after the trial collapsed were those which trapped the private thoughts of ministers like flies in amber. But the most erotically charged for those journalists who get a frisson from this sort of thing are the 'contact notes' of the two intelligence officers, that is, the paperwork generated when the men from MI5 and MI6 met Gutteridge and Henderson respectively, and the 'source reports', which are the distilled essence of those meetings, less any information which might identify the original source. The precautions and care Ford and Balson took not to identify Henderson and Gutteridge now look a little fatuous, given that the Customs prosecution forced both men to 'come out' and declare themselves British spies, to protect the innocence of Abraham, Allen and Henderson himself. There is still the danger of Iraqi retribution, as Ford told the jury.

Top secret these most secret secrets may be, but they are a crushing disappointment to anyone anticipating a good read. Put together and published as a paperback, they would never outsell Catherine Cookson. Their content is often mundane and sometimes plain bizarre. Careful with his words in the witness box, Ford was more forthcoming to his analysts back at the office, spending a great deal of paper describing what he ate and drank when meeting Gutteridge, as if he was a methodical inspector for the *Good Food Guide*. From behind the screen and brown wrapping paper, the image of a ruddy-cheeked gourmand began to emerge. Take the 'SECRET' contact note of a meeting which took place in mid-December 1987: 'drinking tea and munching through the fruit from the bowl in the hotel room . . .' Another busy meeting in late July 1988 goes on till '0300 (with the help of G's brandy).' Perhaps the 'B' in officer B stands for Billy Bunter.

The most striking thing to the casual reader about the body of MI5 and MI6 contact notes and source reports is the amazing amount of blacking out. The classic example is a four-page source report, dated in May 1990 not long before the invasion of Kuwait. On the first page the reader can make out the following words: 'SECRET' in a black-ruled box. Underneath and to the left are two words in capitals: 'SOURCE REPORT'; to the right, in lower case: 'Date information obtained from source' and the precise date. The rest, every single word, has been blacked out with a thick heavy felt-tipped pen. The reader turns the page, breathless. At the top of the second page we find 'SECRET' in a black-lined box. At the bottom, the same. In between? Every single word on every single line has been blacked out. The reader turns the page, breathless. Not a word to be seen, only the censor's heavy black pen, moving to and fro. On the fourth page? Not a word which has not been blacked out. One cannot read such massively redacted documents without the suspicion arising that they are the paper equivalent of the Nixon White House tapes, with the difference that not just the expletives have been deleted.

Nevertheless, there is enough material which has not been deleted in the contact notes and source reports, taken with the later policy documents, to establish without doubt that ministers knew from late 1987 that Matrix Churchill was owned by Iraqis and that it was exporting its machine tools to munitions factories in Iraq.

Ford had a series of meetings with Gutteridge throughout 1987, most often at a Coventry hotel. The agent told Thames Television's *This Week* what the form was: 'I would arrive at the hotel, at the prearranged time, we never met in the reception area. I would go to the reception desk, ask for his name – his cover name – the room number, then I'd go to the room.' Sometimes, when pressed, officer and agent would meet at Gutteridge's home where Mrs Gutteridge cooked dinner. Ford twitters on from time to time about the need to keep her sweet, and even mentions a Christmas present on a contact note, presumably to ensure that there is no difficulty with his MI5 expenses claims. In 1987 Ford met Gutteridge once a month in January, February, March, twice in April. That month Gutteridge met the Iraqis at the offices of the front company, Meed

International, in Duke Street (this Meed should not be confused with the respected *Middle Eastern Economic Digest* magazine), where the machine tools makers were asked to tender for machines to make mortar shells at Habobi's Nassir munitions factory. In a contact note, dated 6 May 1987, Ford minuted that Gutteridge 'told of TI Matrix' – the old company name of Matrix Churchill, before the Iraqis bought it – 'dealings with a London-based Iraqi company. This company is buying milling machines specifically tooled up for arms production.' In June Gutteridge met Ford twice. The same month TI Matrix signed a deal with the Iraqis to supply 120-mm shells for the Nassir munitions factory. In July Gutteridge met Ford three times, once in August, once in September, three times in October – the month Habobi had bought Matrix Churchill – twice in November and twice in December.

The intelligence product from this series of meetings between the Bunteresque MI5 man and Gutteridge was speedily disseminated throughout Whitehall. The unfortunate Coolican, the civil servant who sent the 'dirty washing' minute to Ridley just before the Kuwait invasion, cited how much was known in 1987 as an argument to stop Customs from prosecuting the Matrix Churchill Three. 'Customs have *prima facie* evidence,' he wrote to his secretary of state on 14 June 1990, 'that current machine tools exports from Matrix Churchill and other UK companies are being routed via Chile to Iraq for arms manufacture. Evidence was available in 1987 to the same effect . . .'

The first question to ask is, did Whitehall know who owned Matrix Churchill from October 1987 onwards? The sale of TI Matrix to Habobi was covered in great detail by a source report, dated 28 October 1987, which records the sale of the firm for £6.5 million, the contract being signed on 23 October 1987. The source report then dives into the Habobi maze:

The few original directors at TI have each been invited to purchase £50,000 worth of shares in the new company. This amounts to far less than 20 per cent of the total. TMG own about 90 per cent. TMG is a holding company specially set up to purchase TI Machine Tools. The parent company is TDG (Technical Development Group) which was surreptitiously established by Meed International with money from Iraq, Saudi Arabia and Kuwait . . .

Later, it was registered in Companies House in London – one of the great opennesses of British capitalism – that TDG was owned by al-Arabi Trading Company of Baghdad, a detail Ford missed or did not know at the time.

Ford supplies a 'Source Comment' which is thankfully in plain English: 'It is believed the Iraqi's [sic] are a major shareholder in TDG.' The final line of the source report gives one more clue as to who the true owners were: 'The contract signed by TMG prohibits Matrix Churchill from selling machine tools to either Iran or Israel.'

The second question is, did Whitehall know in 1987 – when the war with Iran was still going on, at the cost of much blood – that machine-tool shipments from Britain were destined for Iraqi munitions factories? During the cross-examination of Tony Steadman, a senior civil servant at the DTI in charge of licensing machine tools for export, Robertson quoted from an intelligence report, dated 30 November 1987, headed 'Iraq: The Procurement of Machinery for Armaments Production'. The report was sent to Steadman, with copies to the Foreign Office and the Ministry of Defence (MOD). Robertson quoted:

According to a British businessman involved in some of the deals, the Iraqi government has been signing contracts with British, West German, Italian and Swiss firms for the purchase of general purpose heavy machinery for the production of armaments in Iraq. Details of those contracts about which the businessman knows are as follows:

(a) TI [a reference to Matrix Churchill's old name] £19 million worth of multispindle and Computer Numerical Control (CNC) lathes . . .

The rest is blacked out. The document as read out by Robertson continues:

> (3) Iraq intends to use the machinery purchased to manu-
> facture its own munitions. According to Anees Wadi of Meed
> International, Iraq has been paying inflated prices for finished
> products from the Soviet Union and now wishes to manufac-
> ture its own cartridges, shell cases, mortars and projectile nose
> cones.
>
> (4) The armament production is to take place in two main
> factories in Iraq: the Hutteen General Establishment for
> Mechanical Industries in Iskandria, and the Nassir General
> Establishment for Mechanical Industries in Taji, near Basra.
> Both factories are large by Western standards and the annual
> production targets for the Nassir factory (the smaller of the
> two) are as follows:
>
> (a) 10,000 122-mm missiles per annum.
>
> (b) 150,000 130-mm shells per annum.
>
> (c) 100,000 mortar shells (60-, 80- and 120-mm) per
> annum.
>
> (d) 300,000 fin-stabilized 155-mm shells per annum (simi-
> lar to those produced by PRB in Belgium).

The document finished, according to Robertson:

> Most of the technical drawings used as blueprints for
> production of the Nassir factory are Russian. The one excep-
> tion noted was a set of American drawings used for a large
> bomb. British businessmen visiting the factory were told that
> it was a 1000-pound bomb. The businessmen were also told
> that all the Soviets had been expelled from the factory.

The eroticism of detail in this intelligence report – copied to
David Mellor's officials at the Foreign Office and Lord Trefgarne's civil servants at the MOD – left Whitehall in no doubt
as to where the machine tools were going.

Despite the seriousness of the work, the British talent for

farce is a constant theme in the documents. Ford had to admit a cock-up to his analysts in late October 1987 when he under-estimated the size of technical drawings Gutteridge had removed from Matrix Churchill at his request. 'Unfortunately (or fortunately, depending on viewpoint) my A4-size photographic equipment was not man enough to cope with 100 sheets of three foot by two foot drawings. If a [deleted] photographer was available, we agreed to repeat the session . . .' His poor agent Gutteridge had to hang on to the drawings for another few days, while a service photographer was produced to do the job properly.

The drawings, some of which had Cyrillic (and therefore were of Russian origin) script on them, were yet more evidence that Matrix Churchill machine tools were going to munitions factories. On 25 November 1987, what appears to be a letter from PO Box 500 – the Whitehall postal address for MI5 – is sent out. The address(es) has been deleted. The letter says: 'Source [deleted] has been able to provide details of the Iraqi contracts with UK companies for general purpose machine tools. Source is in no doubt that all these tools will be used in Iraq for the production of armaments.' Ford agreed in court that the intelligence from Gutteridge was passed on in late November to the relevant Whitehall departments, the DTI, the Foreign Office and the MOD.

On 8 December 1987, Ford wrote up a further source report on the Hutteen General Establishment, which Gutteridge, along with other British businessmen, had visited. Ford records that the visitors were shown the '130-mm shell and mortar shop' and that 'Hutteen staff said that other sizes of shells, cartridges, anti-personnel and anti-tank mines were also manufactured.' It was as plain as a pikestaff that Hutteen, like Nassir, was a munitions factory.

Henderson's barrister, Geoffrey Robertson, would have been failing in his duty not to dwell on this evidence. Long before Alan Clark – prime minister John Major's designated scapegoat, once the case had collapsed – appeared in the witness box, the jury had heard during the cross-examination of Ford that MI5, and by late 1987 the DTI, the Foreign Office and the MOD, were in no doubt that Matrix Churchill was an Iraqi-owned operation shipping machine tools to Iraqi munitions factories.

Just for fun, here are two more pieces of evidence that Whitehall knew in 1987 what was happening. First, the British passed on their intelligence to their American partners. US Congressman Henry Gonzalez investigated the American files and read them into the Congressional Record on 21 September 1992. Gonzalez, the chairman of the House of Representatives banking committee, said:

> Matrix Churchill (Ltd) had contracts to provide machines for Iraq's armaments industry even before it was sold to the Iraqi front company, TDG [in October, 1987].
>
> Matrix had a contract called the ABC contract to supply machines to an Iraqi munitions factory called the Hutteen General Establishment. These machines were to produce 155-mm and 122-mm artillery shells. A second contract, called the ABA contract, was to supply machines to be used in the production of a short-range rocket called the Ababel rocket which was manufactured at the Nassir State Enterprise for Mechanical Industries.

Gonzalez, whose team has spent two years investigating Iraqgate, based his statements on classified US documents dating back to the mid-1980s. He continued:

> The British Department of Trade and Industry approved the deals. The director-general of Hutteen [in Iraq] even had a picture of himself and the British military attaché hanging in his office. That picture was taken during the British miliary attaché's tour of Hutteen.

Second, the DTI sprang into action to stop the shipments. Had they been non-military, why would they have bothered? The DTI action to stop the shipments was to Ford's intense embarrassment as he munched his way through the nearest food source. Robertson read out the contact note, dated 14 December 1987, in open court: ' "Relaxed in our chairs drinking tea and munching through the fruit from the bowl in the hotel room, I believed this was to be one of our routine visits. Unfortunately, when I turned the conversation towards certain subjects it was clear that not all was well. Two days ago" ' – [*Robertson*] 'That is what Mr Gutteridge is telling you [*Ford*] – "two days ago the DTI had telephoned round the companies doing business with Iraq to tell them the export licences could be revoked after all. The DTI caller told TI that 'HMG did not wish to prolong the Gulf War." ' Ford agreed with Robertson that the firm's problem as far as the DTI was concerned was that 'they were going to make munitions which would prolong the Gulf War'.

Henderson told *This Week* that the telephone call came 'from Tony Steadman of the DTI who informed him [a Matrix Churchill manager] that the licences were to be revoked ... mainly because they'd found out that these machine tools were going into munitions-making factories.' The call came in time to stop nearly all the batches of Matrix Churchill lathes going to Iraq.

Gutteridge immediately suspected that it was his intelligence supplied to MI5 that had triggered the threat from the DTI to stop the contracts to Iraq. Gutteridge told the BBC's *Panorama* programme, transmitted 23 November 1992, of the plain speaking between the MI5 man and himself:

> I told him that there would be up to one thousand five hundred jobs at risk, not only with Matrix Churchill, but with other UK machine tool companies. Possibly fifty million pounds' worth of business was at stake. So there were very serous consequences. And it was some time after this report that he told me that the report had landed on the prime minister's desk.

Gutteridge's intelligence, as they like to say, was going right to the very top.

Ford did his best to calm his 'Joe', in John le Carré-speak, and smooth his feathers, but it was an uphill task. Robertson read out to the court what happened next from the contact note.

ROBERTSON: 'After this very tricky period with my nose growing ever longer' – that being a reference to Pinocchio?
FORD: Correct, sir.
ROBERTSON: 'Mr Gutteridge accepted that our meeting could not be held responsible.'

Ford went away, promising to do his best. The conundrum – could the Matrix Churchill shipments to the munitions factories be reconciled with the Howe guidelines? – would tax some of the most resourceful minds in Whitehall. For the moment, the civil servants put the matter on freeze until ministers could make a judgement in the new year.

On 18 November 1987, junior Foreign Office minister David Mellor gave a written reply to a House of Commons question:

> Our policy on defence sales to Iran and Iraq is already one of the strictest of any country, and there are no plans at the present time to introduce further measures. Exports of defence-related equipment are subject to stringent export licensing procedures to ensure they do not contravene the special ministerial guidelines announced in the House on 25 October 1985. We would take a very serious view of any activities in breach of those guidelines.

That year the government licensed a huge volume of defence equipment for export to Iraq, according to details which were finally released to the Commons Trade and Industry Select Committee in November 1991. The exports included gas spectrometers – useful kit for anyone who wants to build himself a nuclear bomb – made at Pye Unicam in Cambridge to the Ministry of Defence, Baghdad; reconditioned jet engines for the Iraqi air force; helicopter engine parts for the Iraqi air force; computers for the Ministry of Defence, Baghdad, and the Iraqi Atomic Energy Commission; a bomb disposal suit for the Ministry of Defence, Baghdad; field artillery computers for the Ministry of Defence, Baghdad; voltage regulators for the Iraqi Atomic Energy Commission; explosives 'for oil well perforating' (perhaps they saved these for blowing up the Kuwaiti oil rigs); encryption and scrambler kits for the Ministry of Defence, Baghdad; Fluorine; night vision rangefinders for the Ministry of Defence, Baghdad; CNC machine tools, from Matrix Churchill (the £19 million order) and other firms, for the munitions factories; pistols, rifles and shotguns for VIP use; plutonium; radio and radio direction-finding kit for the Ministry of Defence, Baghdad; perimeter security system for the 'State organization of Electricity – intruder detection'; tank helmets; thorium oxide for the Nuclear Research Centre; vehicle spares and vehicle radio communications equipment.

Saddam's nose was even longer than Ford's. How could the leader of any country which was party to international treaties guaranteeing human rights explain the Amnesty International report of 1987? As well as the commonplace horrors of torture and execution, that year Amnesty raised the question of what had happened to 300 Kurdish teenagers and children seized by the Iraqi regime from their homes in Sulaimaniya in 1985 and the subsequent execution of a tenth of them. Amnesty reported the evidence of a Kurdish prisoner, himself a victim of torture, who came across some of the 300 at the Fudailiyya Security Headquarters in Baghdad in late 1985. The Amnesty eyewitness gave the following testimony:

. . . we were forbidden to communicate with the children, who were treated with special brutality . . . the cell was so small only a few children could sit down in turn on the floor which was cold and uncovered. The cell was windowless, except for a hole in the door for the security officers to keep watch on us. There was no air to breathe.

Each hour, security men opened the door and chose three to five of the prisoners – children or men – and removed them for torture. Later, their tortured bodies were thrown back into the cell. They were often bleeding and carried obvious signs of whipping and electric shocks. We always tried our best to help them.

At midnight the security men took another three of the children, but because they were so savagely treated they were taken from the cell to a military hospital. It was clear that the security authorities did not wish them to die like this. However, when their wounds were healed, they were returned to the cell.

Some children tried to sleep on the floor. A child who had been in the hospital lay down and finally, we thought, fell asleep. But . . . we knew he was dead. No one knows what happened to his corpse . . .

In January 1987 Amnesty learnt that 29 of the 300 children were believed to have been executed and their bodies returned to their families. According to accounts received by Amnesty, some of the victims had their eyes gouged out and their bodies bore marks of torture. The families were asked to pay a sum of money upon receipt of their bodies – so-called 'execution fees'. The sums requested, Amnesty said, are sometimes several hundred Iraqi dinars per body, and are said to cover state expenses on items such as coffins and, an exquisite touch this, bullets.

On 9 April 1987, the European Parliament passed a resolution expressing its grave concern about the arrest of the 300 children and the execution of 29 of them.

Saddam was unmoved. The war against Iran continued, as did his reign of fear. His ambitions were in no danger of being stymied, because the tyrant could count on those in power throughout the Western capitals. The West, Britain included, spoke more honestly with its money. That September trade minister Alan Clark announced further ECGD credit lines totalling £175 million at the end of Anglo-Iraq trade talks. A DTI press notice, dated 24 September 1987, quoted the minister: 'The new facilities amounted to an expression of confidence in UK/Iraq commercial relations.'

No one mentioned the execution fees.

CHAPTER
THREE

The Old Etonian lifted his fork and lowered it into his glass of champagne, stirring the bubbly until it seethed like a piranha tank at feeding time: 'You get more fizz that way, see?' The Right Honourable Alan Clark is a patrician of the old school, not afraid of stirring things up a little. (Later, elsewhere, I tried Clark's trick. The champagne frothed up, surged over the brim and spilt all over the tablecloth. A waitress passed by and complained: 'Have you been mucking about with the cutlery?') Wilton's, a favourite watering hole of the ruling classes in London's upper-class ghetto, Jermyn Street, was his choice of restaurant. It is discreetly expensive. A 'modest' meal for two costs an arm and two legs. There is no muzak, only the muffled sound of dentures on rolls of freshly baked bread. The waiters are nearly all white, or nearly white.

He was early, a surprisingly slight, slim figure wearing a Toad of Toad Hall waistcoat and blue trousers, his blue eyes glinting intelligence, thin, aquiline face, like a Roman general, still handsome despite the wrinkles. He ordered oysters, nine, turbot, mashed potato, washed down with a few glasses of champagne. He was engagingly indiscreet, savagely funny, hero-ically unstuffy. He reminded me over the oysters and in a couple of telephone conversations of Lord Rothschild's description of Guy Burgess: 'Frightful man; good company.' We both looked forward to the publication of his diaries in the summer of 1993. He promised that the f-word and the w-word occur more often than the run-of-the-mill political memoir. As trade minister in the late eighties he made a habit of collecting tyrants on his trips, for example, he enjoyed meeting General Pinochet in Chile, but unhappily for posterity he did not meet Saddam Hussein when he visited Baghdad for the first and only time in 1986.

How was Baghdad? I asked. 'Matthew Cox, who was in my private office, and I had terrible tummy ache, the worst I have ever had. The food was delicious, but obviously something went wrong. The place was quite creepy. I was very worried at the time about the businessman Ian Richter [arrested in 1986 on trumped-up corruption charges by Saddam's secret police]. I thought, because of my imperialist training, from long before my time at Eton, that when I saw Tareq Aziz [Saddam's foreign minister] they would release him. But no. I found them very sinister and intractable in the small change of diplomacy. The ambassador had not seen any of the key players since he had been there in 1985.'

What about the war?

'Couldn't get butter – the only way you could tell there was a war on.' The tummy upset was so bad that Clark decided once in Baghdad was enough: 'When I came back I said I'm not going to that fucking place again.' It was an option many ordinary Iraqis, similarly minded, could not enjoy.

Clark has taken a great deal of stick from colleagues in the Conservative Party, including prime minister John Major who identified him in a speech to the House of Commons, as the culprit in the Iraqgate scandal. The chief charge against Clark is that he changed his line in the witness box during the Matrix Churchill case from his earlier witness statement to Customs investigators. It is an accusation which Clark rebuts and the evidence does not support.

But blaming Clark was an easy line for the government to run, because of his iridescent public image: 'High profile, you see. Have a bright plumage, people take pot shots at you,' he said stoically. He is the son of Lord Clark of *Civilization* fame, the television documentary series that brought Culture to the broad masses. Clark Junior – as he would never be called – is also a man of fine tastes and has the money to indulge them. The family wealth comes from Paisley thread manufacture, wisely invested to make Clark, when he was in the Commons, the subject of some envy from the poorer tribunes. One gibe was that Clark was 'like Ghenghis Khan, only richer'. His country home, Saltwood Castle in Kent, has fifty rooms and is the place where the wicked knights conspired to do away with the 'troublesome priest', Thomas à Becket. There are also a London flat, a couple of other houses and a 27,000-acre estate of rolling heather in Sutherland. Every now and then he flogs one of the pictures hanging on the walls of one of his homes to tide him over. The last one to go was a Turner in 1984 to pay capital transfer tax. The sale raised £7.4 million. He is entertaining about his wealth. 'I don't need to get any richer,' he told the *House* magazine in 1984. 'Once you've got a certain amount of money, you are really better off living on the income, or preferably on the income of the income.'

Eton was nasty. He said of his school years that it was a unique introduction to 'human cruelty, treachery and extreme physical hardship'. At Oxford the sharpness of his mind started to be noticed. He became an '*homme serieux*', though there was also a novel – *Bargains at Special Prices* – which, despite the echo in the title, is not about flogging machine tools to make bombs on the cheap to Middle-Eastern dictators. He matured to become a historian in his own right with a string of acerbic, controversial but strongly argued books to his name. His lasting gift to British culture is *The Donkeys*, a superb stiletto job on the incompetence of generals Haig, French and Dorian Smith, who did for the prime of British youth in 1915. At least one admiring journalist has noticed the strange paradox of Clark the creature of privilege crystallizing in the public mind the rotten nature of privilege when in power. *The Donkeys* shows that the ordinary British Tommies really were 'lions led by donkeys'. The book provoked Joan Littlewood to produce *Oh What a Lovely War*, the sharp satire on the follies and tragedies of the First World War as seen through the music hall. Although Clark has expressed some irritation at the more sentimental 'lefty' aspects of the play, which was later made into a film by Sir Richard Attenborough, he became firm friends with Littlewood and enjoyed its success. Over the oysters, we sang some of the songs from *Oh What a Lovely War*, including the line from 'We Are Fred Kano's Army':

> The Kaiser he did say:
> 'Hoch! Hoch! Mein Gott!
> What a fucking rotten lot
> Are the ragtime infantry . . .

to the mild consternation of fellow diners. He likes nothing better than to '*épater* the bourgeoisie'.

Further evidence that he does not have a conventional thought in his head came with *Barbarossa – the Russo-German Conflict 1941–1945*. In the second edition of this book, first published in 1965, he expressed remorse at showing too much indignation at German atrocities. 'Now I see the [German] rejection of the Judaeo-Christian ethic as part of a yearning for the primitivism of the Teutonic Knights . . . It is a recurrent theme in the history of that great nation whose denial does its people no credit and diminishes from their culture.' The journalist Donald Macintyre in an otherwise sympathetic profile in the *Independent* wondered aloud: 'Is this a serious pat on the back for the Germanic ideal which decayed into Nazism – or just another attempt to shock?'

The idea of Clark in Nazi jodhpurs has been given more credence by his pronouncements on race. In 1972 he said that the Ugandan Asians, fleeing Idi Amin's tyranny, should be told: 'You cannot come into this country because you are not white.' In 1984 he was accused of having made a remark in a private meeting about 'Bongo-Bongo Land'. Unpleasant, yes, but these views are not very different from those of some of his colleagues. Over lunch we discussed the career of Lord Young, his former boss. I made some remark disparaging his record, but Clark was quick to stand up for him, adding that 'David had suffered because of anti-semitism in the party' – a remark which does not square with those who would paint Clark in the worst light possible.

In January 1993 he came out in favour of the revisionist view of the Second World War, warmly receiving a new book by young historian John Charmley, who claimed that Churchill had blundered by not making peace with Hitler in 1941. Personally, I find this view obnoxious but on this and other matters Clark is consistent and willing to state his case in public. He said over the oysters that the West 'would have been immeasurably better off had the Germans and the Russians fought themselves to a standstill'.

On the page, Clark has written of the 'bewitching' idea of Nazism. But in the flesh, in conversation, he is far too open to ideas, too democratic, to make a convincing Nazi. Far from being a Nazi, Clark came across as an Old Etonian version of the sort of elitist but honourable and recklessly brave Prussian aristocrats who tried to kill Hitler in the summer of 1944. This is a compliment which I would not choose to make of some of the other characters in this narrative.

Clark does not see himself as the guilty party in the Iraqgate scandal. Although he wants to defend his reputation he is also anxious because of the old tribal vows of the Conservative Party not to 'rat' on the others. 'I am the chaff that they put out to keep others off the hunt.'

He expressed himself, perhaps a little too forcefully, on the usefulness of the Scott inquiry to Peter Lennon, in the *Guardian*, on 9 January 1993: 'The moment you announce an inquiry the thing's dead. Who gives a toss about the findings? They are not yesterday's fish and chips but last February's fish and chips.'

Clark has also been dismissed as being disloyal to his colleagues. He is, however, endearingly loyal to Margaret Thatcher, whom he calls 'Her' or 'The Lady'. Lennon asked in the *Guardian*: 'Was she very attractive, very sexy?' Clark replied: 'Very attractive. Sexually. I have never come across any other woman in politics as attractive. In terms of eyes, wrists. Her ankles.'

Unlike some of his colleagues Clark's position on trade with dictatorship has always been consistent. His view is that there are so many nasty dictatorships around the world that UK Ltd cannot afford to be choosy. He argued this line in confidence, within Whitehall; he argued the same line in public, even daring to face a hanging court in the form of a Channel 4 late night show. The Matrix Churchill trial was treated to a read-through of the confrontation between Clark, playing himself, and a Channel 4 presenter, played by Rumpole of the Bailey look-alike Gilbert Gray. The exchanges were prefigured by Clark having a crack at the presenter. Gray misunderstood the sex of the presenter.

GRAY: It is Miss Gove, is it, who did the interviewing?

CLARK: Mr – or Master, he was.

GRAY: Master. Is that because of the 'Ms' you say that?

CLARK: No. He was a juvenile . . . (Laughter.)

GRAY: (*reading from the programme transcript*): 'This October we welcomed three Indonesian officers to our shores to show up on their soldiering skills and while they study their comrades continue the slow extermination of the East Timorese . . . With me, to defend the practice is Alan Clark . . . Do you think it is right that we should actually train Indonesian army officers that have been responsible for slaughtering nearly a quarter of the population of an island independent until '75?' Then, perhaps you would like to read the parts that you took?

CLARK: Yes. I will read them. 'I shouldn't think anyone in the audience knows where East Timor is on the map. Well, do you?'

GRAY: 'I would have to say, Mr Clark, if they are ignorant . . . of its whereabouts, that is probably due to your Conservative education policies.'

CLARK: That set the tone for our exchanges . . .

GRAY: 'But nevertheless, a lot of the people died and the army that has killed them has had officers trained in this country. Do you think that is fair?'

CLARK: 'It is total hypocrisy. This line of yours is total hypocrisy. Have you read the Amnesty report on India? Let us see a TV programme on India. India has child slavery, and a caste system, and every kind of exploitation. There are about three or maybe four countries in the world where human rights are respected: Britain, Australia, New Zealand, maybe Sweden. I do not know, and after that it tails off. Just to pick on one country and say, "Oh, you know, we should not be supplying this." What's going on here? And why are we suddenly fixing on East Timor? I mean, there is no one here who knows where East Timor is. There certainly isn't anyone here who knows anyone who has come from East Timor . . .'

Inside and outside Whitehall, Clark argued that what mattered was British jobs. This is a perfectly valid argument, but not the one the British government as a whole chose to advance. Rather, the official line was that Britain followed the Howe guidelines, a seeming but phoney deference towards morality in trade.

It was not East Timor but Iraq which appeared in the ministers' red boxes in the new year of 1988. Clark at the DTI, David Mellor, the junior minister at the Foreign Office, Lord Trefgarne at the MOD and their civil servants had to decide whether to allow the shipments from Matrix Churchill and the other companies, worth in total £37 million, to go to the Iraqi munitions factories or not. Matrix Churchill had already managed to ship 13 lathes, but 141 machine tools valued at £19 million remained in Britain, waiting for the word from Whitehall.

The killing had not stopped. At the turn of the year the war between Iraq and Iran was still bitterly contested, but both sides were bloodied and punch-drunk. Saddam had been under great pressure in the early years, after his 'blitzkrieg' invasion of Iran had rebounded in his face. Iraq had started to sag underneath Iran's greater numbers and the human wave attacks by the Shia teenagers, brain-washed to equate 'Paradise' with the Iraqi front lines. But Iranian advances had been checked by Saddam's use of poison gas from 1984 onwards. The Iraqis bedded down behind monstrous defences, repelling Iranian attacks which lost thousands of lives for yards of soil gained – a terrible echo of British offensive strategy in First World War battles like the

Somme, castigated by Clark in *The Donkeys*. Britain and the West were happy to see both sides slog it out, until the Iraqi defences snapped and the Iranians swarmed over the Fao peninsula in 1986. The Iranians' victory was partly due to the shot in the arm provided by the up-to-date weapons, including TOW missiles, authorized by Colonel Oliver North, seeking to swap arms for the Western hostages held by Iran's friends, the Shia Hezbollah, in the Lebanon.

The loss of the Fao peninsula caused the West to panic. The US State Department and the British Foreign Office were terrified of the Islamic fundamentalists threatening the oil monarchies beyond Iraq. From the fall of the Fao peninsula, Whitehall's decision-making has to be seen in the context of the West's tilt to Iraq. And Iraq's repeated abuses of human rights and its flagrant violations of the ban on chemical weapons? The West looked the other way.

By the beginning of 1988 Iraq held the upper hand, gaining ground because it was in receipt of a wave of Western arms and technology with which it could prosecute the war and because Saddam could use poison gas without fear of any effective sanction. The Ayatollah Khomeini, on the other hand, had forbidden the use of chemical weapons by the Iranians because of a Koranic verse outlawing the poisoning of the environment.

It was against this background that the three ministers and their civil servants went into battle. The Foreign Office view, based on the MI5 intelligence reports and MI6 analysis, was to stop the shipments. The DTI was all in favour of Britain securing as much trade as possible. The MOD had no tilt on the matter, but was anxious not to let the Iraqis have any kit too new, lest it fall into Soviet hands. Tony Steadman, the director of the DTI's export licensing unit – who gave evidence at the trial – started attacking the Foreign Office line. He wrote to the MOD on 13 January 1988, arguing that the shipments did not in fact breach the guidelines. They were not enhancing the Iraqi war effort – part of the Howe test – because the British machine tools were making up for a shortfall in Soviet supplies. There was another chink of light for the DTI, first glimpsed by Matrix Churchill's commercial manager, Trevor Abraham. He had 'suggested that not all the machines would be used on munitions'.

What Whitehall feared most of all was that the row would attract unfavourable publicity, making it much more difficult to let the shipments go. Civil servant Bill Morgan laid to rest any pretension to open government on 13 January 1988: 'There seems to be considerable merit in keeping as quiet as possible about this politically sensitive issue . . . although . . . we should be aware that news of this kind is likely to leak and ministers should therefore be forewarned.' Morgan argued that 'we should be very careful about the validity of the claims of munitions manufacture', fearing mischief-making by foreign competitors for the Iraqi contracts, but he also recognized the unpalatable truth: '. . . while at the same time be aware that almost any machine tool supplied to a country at war will eventually be used to support that war effort in some form or other.'

That everyone should keep mum was Steadman's advice to Clark prior to him meeting a delegation which included Paul Henderson from the Machine Tool Trades Association (MTTA) on 20 January 1988. This wisdom was reinforced by Steadman's boss, assistant secretary Eric Beston, who added in his own hand: 'The need for a low profile by MTTA companies is important. We not wish to face the FCO [Foreign and Commonwealth Office] with "presentational difficulties".'

If any pupils at Sunningdale, Britain's school for mandarins, are ever taught that the civil service is not a conspiracy to conceal the truth from the public in order to serve the partisan needs of the party in power then they should quote back at their teachers the Matrix Churchill case.

Beston's performance in the witness box struck reporters as that of the perfect functionary. Saucery eyes, received diction, a mind that runs on casters. Smooth manner, smoother face – for a mandarin like Beston smoothness is all. It was, of course, more than a little embarrassing for Beston when Robertson mercilessly made him read out his *obiter dicta*: 'The need for a low profile . . .' in open court. Robertson was in fine form when he tightened the thumb screws on the functionary.

ROBERTSON: That again is the FCO. I think Mr David Mellor
was the minister at the time?
BESTON: I think so.

Extraordinary, really, that an assistant secretary who joined
the DTI in 1975 should be the slightest part uncertain about
what job Mellor had. A few months earlier Mellor had been
taken to task by an opposition MP for 'ego-tripping' from TV
studio to studio to speak on the Middle East crisis. In January
1988 he made headline news around the world for tearing into
an Israeli army officer in the Gaza Strip for 'inhumanity' towards
Palestinian Arabs.
The silk gave a further turn of the screw.

ROBERTSON: You didn't wish to face him with embarrassing
publicity or publicity that would embarrass him with the
revalidation or the continuance of these licences?
BESTON: I didn't want to face ministers generally with embarrassment which might push the decision in one direction
rather than another. I wanted to leave it open.

Clark made a good impression on the machine tool makers,
particularly Henderson, who said in a break during the trial after
Clark had given evidence: 'I respected him then and I respect
him now.' The MTTA kept minutes of the meeting, which
recorded Clark's advice to the businessmen: 'The intended use of
the machines should be couched in such a manner as to
emphasize the peaceful aspect to which they should be put.
Applications should stress the record of "general engineering"
usage of machine tools.'
It was a classic instance of Whitehall's version of the card
sharp's game 'Find the Lady'. They knew the machine tools were
going to munitions factories thanks to the intelligence from
Gutteridge. It was easier to step around the Howe guidelines if
Whitehall forgot that intelligence and everybody emphasized 'the
general engineering' description. As the civil servants shuffled
the pack of words, no one would be able to find the munitions
factories in the blur.

In court, Robertson's cross-examination of Clark led to an enrichment of the English language.

ROBERTSON: But here the writer of this minute is attributing to you a statement – 'The Iraqis will be using the current order for general engineering purposes' – which cannot be correct to your knowledge.

CLARK: Well, it's our old friend 'being economical', isn't it?

ROBERTSON: With the truth?

CLARK: With the *actualité*.

Clark was thus finessing the original formulation, by Cabinet secretary Sir Robert Armstrong who told the Spycatcher trial that the British government had been 'economical with the truth'. Later, Clark gave a nice definition of *actualité*: instant truth. But, for the moment, the former minister continued.

CLARK: There was nothing misleading or dishonest to make a formal or introductory comment that the Iraqis would be using the current orders for general engineering purposes. All I didn't say was 'and for making munitions'.

If the best and brightest of the civil service were doing peculiar things to the language to allow the shipments to go ahead, the press does not emerge altogether unscathed from this episode in the saga. During the famous 20 January meeting one of the machine tool makers said the *Daily Telegraph* had caught a sniff of the story. Robertson reminded Clark of the exchange.

ROBERTSON: And I think you said, or the recollection of one of those attending is that you said, 'Well, I will get on to the editor of the *Daily Telegraph*. He is a friend of mine.'

CLARK: Yes . . .

ROBERTSON: Did you in fact get on to the editor?

CLARK: Yes.

ROBERTSON: And we see Mr Gribben's article is at page 32. [The article, headlined 'Ministers split on £50m machine tools for Iraq' by Roland Gribben was placed on the business pages.]

So you were not able to stop the article appearing but you were able perhaps to give it a definite anti-Foreign Office slant?

There was laughter in court when Clark replied in his patrician drawl: 'That would not be difficult.'

But Britain is not Iraq. The report appeared somewhere in the *Daily Telegraph*. The journalist was not executed.

Although Clark was the lead minister, Lord Trefgarne at the MOD and David Mellor at the Foreign Office knew what was going on. 'PS Mr Mellor' – that is, Mellor's PS or private secretary – is written at the top of the Foreign Office distribution list by an unknown hand for a critical briefing paper from Bill Patey of the Foreign Office's Middle East Department, dated 28 January 1988. Another name on the distribution list is Sir David Miers, the permanent under-secretary at the Foreign Office. Patey ran through the arguments in favour of arming the Iraqis 'now that we have information that the consignee will use them to manufacture munitions'.

The most damaging minute of all came from the MOD civil servant Allan Barrett. He wrote:

> We have obtained intelligence, believed by the DIS [Defence Intelligence Staff] to be reliable, that the lathes are to go to munitions factories to produce missiles and shells in large quantities. Had this information been available at the time the licence applications were considered, the MODWG [Ministry of Defence Working Group] would have advised the IDC [Inter-Departmental Committee (of civil servants looking at defence exports to Iran and Iraq)] that the military assessment was that the use of the lathes for this purpose would constitute a significant enhancement in Iraq's capability to prolong the conflict with Iran.

The MOD's initial view was that the machine tools shipments to Iraqi munitions factories represented a plain breach of the Howe guidelines. But Barratt went on to cite both the Russian – the British lathes were merely replacing Soviet shells – and the 'general engineering' defences in favour of shipment. The Howe guidelines were fizzing at the edges as the civil servants lowered them into the Whitehall acid-bath.

Patey exploited the Soviet defence to the full. He wrote in the minute distributed to David Mellor's private secretary:

> It is likely that had we known from the outset that the machine tools would be used to manufacture munitions we would have recommended that licences be refused. At present the Iraqis import most of their shells from the Soviet Union. The Iraqi aim is to replace this supply with local manufacture. It is therefore arguable that the Iraqi capability will not be significantly enhanced.

In the House of Commons debate on Iraqgate on 23 November 1992, the Liberal foreign affairs spokesman David Steel quoted that extract from Patey and commented: 'That gives the game away. If one argues that because Iraq intends to manufacture its own shells with equipment that we supply it is therefore merely replacing Russian imports and its capability is not being enhanced, the guidelines are, of course, beautifully observed.' So we did not arm Iraq. We sold them the tools to arm themselves.

A few days later, the DTI's freeze on the shipments thawed overnight. The individual firms were informed by telephone. But, perhaps not very surprisingly, no written note of the decision has been disclosed to show that Mellor, Clark and Trefgarne, acting on the advice of their civil servants, decided to unfreeze the shipments. Geoffrey Robertson pursued the matter when he cross-examined the DTI civil servant Beston.

ROBERTSON: When did the ministers [Mellor, Clark and Trefgarne, previously identified] to your recollection approve the continuance of the licences?

BESTON: Um, as far as I can recall it would have been early February that year, 1988.

ROBERTSON: If we look at ... the minutes ... 'it was understood that ministers had agreed that the licences should not be revoked'. And that is a minute on the 19th February, 1988?

BESTON: Yes.

ROBERTSON: . . . We have no document that has been disclosed to indicate how or when this decision came down to you. So I will have to ask you from memory to tell us whether you recall in this period some indication from your minister, Mr Alan Clark, that the licences you describe as being frozen could be unfrozen? Can you recall how it happened?

BESTON: Um, no I can't . . .

Was it a case of 'now they break the guidelines, now they don't'?

But no minister cared to share their Jesuitry with the House of Commons or the public at the time they took their decision in 1988. David Mellor wrote to Labour MP Ken Eastham on 9 March 1988, declaring: 'We prohibit the sale of any defence related equipment that could significantly enhance the capability of either side to prolong or exacerbate the conflict. This policy is enforced by a strict export licence regime and all applications are rigorously scrutinized.'

Mellor's reply is beautifully tailored given that he was on the distribution list for Patey's minute of 28 January 1988, which baldly stated the problem over the machine tools 'now that we have information that the consignee will use them to manufacture munitions'.

A more frank reply by Mellor to the MP would have gone something like this: 'We have recently approved the shipment of £37 million worth of machine tools to manufacture munitions. We do not think this valuable trade will significantly enhance the capability of Iraq to prolong or exacerbate the conflict.'

The torture of the English language conducted by ministers was carried out with the full knowledge and help of their sometimes queasy civil servants. One of the language-torture gang, Mark Higson, was a first secretary on the Iraq desk at the Foreign Office, before he left, disillusioned, a few months before Saddam invaded Kuwait.

Over a pint of Pedigree and a packet of salt and vinegar crisps – considerably cheaper than oysters and bubbly at Wilton's – Higson explained the art with which the Howe guidelines were drawn up. 'Look at the phrasing of it,' he said. 'Take that phrase "significantly enhance the capability of either side to prolong or exacerbate the conflict". The key word, open to our interpretation, is "significantly". You can do a lot with that.'

The folly of arming Saddam Hussein was made clear by another event that took place on that fateful day, 20 January 1988, when Alan Clark was 'economical' with the tool makers. Abdullah Rahim Sharif Ali, an Iraqi businessman who worked in London, was admitted to St Stephen's Hospital, Chelsea, with chest problems. He died the same day. The coroner for inner West London found that Ali had been 'unlawfully killed' by thallium poison. According to the journalist Simon Henderson in his book *Instant Empire* (San Francisco: Mercury House, 1991) Ali told police on his deathbed that he had been visited by three Iraqis, who had taken him out to dinner at a London restaurant. He had tasted nothing. Thallium is odourless, tasteless and colourless. A lot of people were suffering from thallium poisoning that month. According to a report in *The Times*, 13 January 1988, an Iraqi Mata Hari used it to poison a meeting of Kurdish leaders. Her family were being held hostage by Saddam's torturers in Baghdad. More than forty Kurds were poisoned. Six died.

Thallium is said to be a favourite method of assassination for Saddam's men. It has another use.

Rat poison.

CHAPTER
FOUR

'Choo-choo! Choo-choo! Choo-choo!' (*Sound effects.*)

A gravy train pulls into Baghdad station disgorging the Right Honourable Members. An Iraqi porter helps one of the MPs struggling with his bags. The porter is a rough, salt-of-the-earth type who speaks with a Cockney accent.

PORTER: This way for the photo-call with the mass-murdering Saddam Hussein! This way for the free fudge! Oops! Mind how you go, sir. Who left that corpse there? (*Honourable Member steps over corpse, holding his nose.*) Come along. This way for the free Saddam Hussein Mickey Mouse watch! You want to what, sir? See the steam engines. Fine, but no questions about human rights, please. This way for the free Aladdin's lamp! (*Exeunt.*)

Such might be the opening scene if any of our leading satirical playwrights cared to write a black comedy about a freebie by a group of British MPs to Baathist Iraq. Howard Brenton and David Hare, the authors of *Pravda*, might have some fun with the Baghdad gravy train, dreaming up all sorts of improbable nonsense, with Honourable Members offered free gifts and rides in air-conditioned limousines as, not so far away, poor wretches screamed in agony in the tyrant's torture chambers. A little fanciful? As they say, the truth is always stranger than fiction.

The Right Honourable Members flew into Saddam Hussein International Airport on 19 February 1988. It was dark, but even so they were met on the airport tarmac by a high-powered Iraqi delegation, the British ambassador and various flunkeys, before their motorcade departed for the Al Rashid Hotel in downtown Baghdad.

They were a motley crew, led by Anthony 'Tony' Rivers Marlow, the Conservative member for Northampton North, on a short fact-finding tour of the Middle East, culminating with Iraq. With him in the motorcade were ten other members, six more Tories and three Labour.

According to Dr Omar Al-Hassan, of the Gulf Centre for Strategic Studies, who organized the trip, the Tories were Robert Adley, the member for Christchurch, Michael Brown, the member for Brigg and Cleethorpes, Nicholas Budgen, the member for Wolverhampton South West, Robert Hicks, the member for Cornwall South-East, Roger Moate, the member for Faversham, and Richard Page, the member for Hertfordshire South West. The Labour MPs were John Cummings, the member for Easington, Robert Parry, the member for Liverpool, Riverside, and David Young, the member for Bolton South-East. Parliament's *Register of Members' Interests* records the 1988 visits by nearly all the MPs. John Cummings does not mention the trip in 1989, '90, '91, or '92 Registers. Cummings said, 'I'm non-plussed that it was not in the Register. It must have been an oversight.' (A Conservative MP, named by Dr Al-Hassan, does not mention a subsequent trip made in 1989 in the 1990, '91, or '92 Registers.)

At the time of the trip Marlow was a consultant to the Gulf Centre for Strategic Studies. He filed the free visit in the 1989 *Register* as follows: 'trip to Kuwait, Bahrein and Iraq in spring 1988 at the invitation of national governments'. (Some of the other MPs said they had been the guests of the Gulf Centre for Strategic Studies.) According to Roth's *Parliamentary Profiles*, this was not Marlow's first free trip to the Arab world. He visited Jordan and the West Bank as PLO guest in January and February 1981; visited Yasser Arafat as guest of the Arab League in February 1984; visited Lebanon as guest of the Druze community in March 1984; visited Baghdad as guest of the

Iraqi government in July 1984; visited West Bank and Gaza as guest of the Arab League, October 1984; visited Tunis as guest of an Arab organization in December 1987; visited West Bank, Gaza and Jordan as guest of an Arab organization, September 1988; and visited Iraq again, invitation from Arab sources, September 1989.

Adley is by his own admission a 'railway lunatic', the author of *The Call of Steam*, 1982, *In Praise of Steam*, 1985 and other threnodies to steam engines (the relevance of this information will soon become apparent).

Michael Brown is, according to *Parliamentary Profiles*, an 'assiduous free-tripper'. The guidebook to MPs cites the following evidence. Brown went to Taiwan as a guest of the Anti-Communist League for World Freedom Day in 1984; to Namibia at the expense of its then South African-sponsored regime in January 1985; to North Cyprus as guest of Turkish-Cypriot President Denktash in March 1985; to the USA as a guest of the US Foreign Policy Council in April 1985; to Israel as a guest of the Conservative Friends of Israel in January 1986; to South Africa as a guest of the South African government in April 1986; to Iceland as a guest of Fylkir Ltd and Grimsby Town Football Club in August 1986; to USA as guest of US Tobacco Inc., in September 1986; and to Bophutatswana – a curious black homeland 'state' with a white South African defence minister – as a guest of its president, Lucas Mangope, in September 1987.

According to *Parliamentary Profiles* Hicks is the 'leading Arab free-tripper'. Roth's guide cites the following evidence. He visited Oman as a guest of its government in December 1983; visited the USA as guest of the Council for Arab-British Understanding in March 1984; visited Iraq as guest of Gulf Research Centre, April 1984; visited South Africa as guest of the South African Sports Foundation, May to June 1984; visited Jordan as guest of Arab League, November 1984; visited Norway and Sweden for the Parliamentary Association for Euro-Arab Co-operation, October 1985; visited Jordan, West Bank and Gaza as guest of the Arab League, August 1986; visited Norway and Sweden for the Parliamentary Association for Euro-Arab Co-operation, March

1987; visited the PLO Council in Algiers, as guest of the Arab League, April 1987; visited the West Bank as guest of Parliamentary Association for Euro-Arab Co-operation, February 1988; then the trip to Kuwait, Bahrein and Iraq; visited North Cyprus as guest of its 'Turkish Republic', April 1988; visited Iran on a conciliation visit initiated by the Archbishop of Canterbury, June 1988; visited Syria with others as a guest of the Syrian government, against UK government opposition, October 1988.

The party had been on a tour of the Middle East before they arrived in Baghdad; Cummings joined the trip in Baghdad. In Bahrein, according to Robert Adley, 'We had a very sumptuous watch given by the Sheikh of Bahrein.' Dr al-Hassan said the watch was, from memory, Swiss-made and worth more than £1000. To give some idea of its value, Dr al-Hassan said the duty payable on the watch back at Heathrow was £112.

It would be quite wrong to describe the trip as a holiday. On the contrary, the MPs' diaries were packed with meetings with ministers and functionaries where they were told Iraq's version of world events. There was a humanitarian dimension to the trip, as Roger Moate explained: 'Our main wishes were for the release of two British hostages.' They were Ian Richter and John Smith. The MPs were given a full briefing by the British ambassador and were left in no doubt as to the nature of the regime. The MPs paid their respects at the tomb of the Unknown Soldier in Baghdad. Marlow's slow march at the shrine was much admired, according to Nick Budgen: 'In congratulating the Iraqis for their courage, he spoke as a soldier, the son of a soldier and the father of soldier.'

Marlow recalled: 'It is important to note that these things were cleared with the Foreign Office and it [visiting Iraq] was looked upon at the time as being in the interests of the UK. In a way, it was like a low-level diplomatic mission, because for various reasons we wanted to keep the lines open to Iraq. While we were there, we had dinner at the Ambassador's residence and various Iraqis were asked along to that dinner, and also British business people had been invited along.'

It was not all hard slog, however. Marlow gave a joking

reply when asked what the MPs did in the evenings: 'Oh, they provided us with women!' He laughed. 'No! We went to an old building in the centre of Baghdad and we had a meal there.' Roger Moate recalled 'a splendid evening with local politicians at what seemed like an ancient hostelry'. Richard Page said: 'They put on a "cultural evening" for us – lots of people coming on to a stage and scraping peculiar-sounding instruments.' He added quickly: 'No belly-dancing orgies.'

The day came when the MPs went to see Saddam. They were driven to the cavernous presidential palace in a motorcade of Mercedes Benz limousines. The MPs went through tight security, passing police and officers of the Republican Guard standing on street corners.

Marlow was asked what were his impressions of Saddam: 'He's got a great presence of personality, a very forceful and shrewd individual . . . Don't let it be said that I'm a supporter of his or that I support his aims and objectives or his methods, because I'm certainly not saying that.' Did Marlow raise human rights issues with Saddam? 'When we were there, one of the party raised human rights issues at one of the meetings that we went to, but the purpose at the time – which was obviously before the Gulf conflict blew up – was to get to know Iraq and the Iraqis and what was happening there. I mean we were well aware of, and had our views on, human rights, but it wouldn't have actually served the purpose of the visit to have taken any particular line on that at that time. That wasn't what we were doing.'

Roger Moate again: 'Before we met him we'd already been briefed about his rather murky reputation – reported murders and so on – so one went into an atmosphere that was rather forbidding. The military protection was extreme. He was obviously very charismatic, very tall . . . a very powerful man, but very charming and courteous.'

There was one disconcerting edge towards Saddam's charm and courtesy, however, as Moate said: 'The overwhelming memory is of him and all his cabinet ministers sporting revolvers.'

It was second time around for Robert Hicks, who first met Saddam in 1981. Of the 1988 meeting Hicks recalled 'a frightening thug. His presence is massive. You're very conscious he is in the room. He was always surrounded by a group of heavies which is very disconcerting. He's got a certain charm – let's not underestimate that. You're conscious very much of his position, that is, the leader in a highly centralized police state. Even when you are participating in a normal conversation, you are a little uneasy.'

It was Saddam's eyes that got to Richard Page. 'I said to my wife that he had one of the hardest pair of eyes that I've ever seen. They were just flat black discs. I thought this is a guy who had absolutely no feelings whatsoever. If he had a sense of humour, he didn't show it at our meeting.'

Cummings said Saddam was 'an absolutely horrifying figure. He just oozed wickedness. Cobra eyes. A really fearful creature.'

Saddam spent the meeting making his usual pitch about the evils of the Iranian enemy; the war was still going strong, but now to the Iraqis' favour, partly because of their use of poison gas.

At their audience with Saddam, one might have expected the visitors from the Mother of Parliaments to raise the tyrant's systematic abuse of human rights; his reign of state terror; the amply documented cases of torture, mutilation and sadism towards innocent men, women and children at the mercy of the various organs of state security. Page said: 'Saddam was wearing a revolver on his hip. It was sheer common sense not to mention anything. When dealing with different races, you take it [human rights issues] more gently.'

Michael Brown agreed that raising human rights abuses to Saddam would not have been appropriate. 'I thought then that I wouldn't want to be on the wrong side of him. He had a gun in his holster. We were courteous and polite and very careful about going in all guns blazing.'

Parry, Dr al-Hassan and Budgen also said that no one discussed human rights with Saddam. Adley confirmed that the MPs were on their best behaviour: 'We were watching our Ps and Qs. He had a gun, a revolver.' Cummings recalled that in the meeting with Saddam 'the conversation touched, skirted around, human rights', though he personally did not have occasion to mention them to the President.

The MPs undoubtedly used every opportunity to press for the release of the British hostages. Dr al-Hassan remembered that 'Nicholas Pigeon' – his Middle-Eastern accent doing an injustice to Budgen – 'raised' human rights with some of the Iraqis, but not Saddam himself. No doubt the others did raise human rights matter where they felt it appropriate.

It is a pity that it proved difficult to make a sustained presentation to the tyrant himself about Iraq's abuse of human rights. One wonders who else would be in a position to register the international community's distaste for the Iraqi regime's routine use of torture, execution, abduction and poison gas than a Member of Parliament from the world's oldest and most robust democracy. Certainly not Saddam's terrified people. Had one of the eleven MPs asked a question about human rights, Saddam would hardly have taken him out and assassinated him on the spot, as he did his health minister, Riyadh Ibrahim. He was not yet ready for a second Gulf War.

Robert Adley did brave one direct request. Because of the ubiquitous and paranoid security in Iraq, his hosts had repeatedly thwarted Adley's desire to see the steam engines of Iraqi railways. 'Not possible. Danger of spies,' they had told him. So Adley popped the question to the strong man himself. Could he see Baghdad's steam engines? 'It was the only time he laughed,' Adley said. Saddam graciously acceded to the Honourable Member's polite request.

For his courage, Adley was rewarded with a tour around the shunting yards of the Baghdad East railway station, while the rest of the party went on a tour of Nebuchadnezzar's Babylon, as rebuilt by the contemporary strong man. 'Most of the Iraqi stock runs on standard gauge,' the train-spotter said breathlessly, 'but there is some metre gauge. There were some 4-6-0s still in working condition, in steam . . . I collect trophies wherever I go. I got a manufacturer's plate off a 1910 vintage 4-6-0 and an early

1950s 2-6-4 tank engine. [Readers who are not up on their train lore might care to know that a 'tank engine' in this context is a sort of locomotive, not a machine of war.] I also got a manufacturer's plate from a Cowan Sheldon steam crane and an absolutely enormous spanner.'

But like a plot twist in one of the Reverend W. Awdry's *Thomas the Tank Engine* stories all was not well in the Iraqi shunting yards when a bright shiny new engine steamed in, full of puff. And the name of the brash new engine? David Mellor.

The foreign office minister with responsibility for the Middle East arrived in Baghdad while the parliamentary delegation was doing the rounds. Anglo-Iraq relations were on the up. Mellor had just taken part in the decision to unfreeze the machine tools that were going to Saddam's munitions factories from Matrix Churchill and the other companies. But he was in Baghdad on a mission: to win the freedom of John Smith, a British prisoner. Smith, who worked for vehicle manufacturer Hestair Dennis, was arrested in 1979 in a Baghdad park with an Iraqi. Four Iraqis who stood trial with him on charges of corruption were later executed, including the mayor of Baghdad who had been Mellor's host on a previous trip to Iraq.

Mellor came to Baghdad bearing a letter from the then prime minister, Margaret Thatcher, pleading for Smith's release. Earlier pleas for Smith's return had foundered when the Iraqis suggested a swap with the hitman arrested in London for the killing of the former prime minister, Abdul Razzaq al-Nayef, in July 1978. Saddam graciously acceded to Mellor's request.

No one mentioned in the newspapers that Britain had earlier that year agreed to export its technology to Iraqi munitions factories.

Nevertheless, it would be churlish not to acknowledge Mellor's diplomatic coup. John Smith's family were delighted. His wife tasted champagne – her first alcoholic drink since her husband's arrest. *The Times* reported: 'Mellor clinches Iraqi pardon for jailed director.' The *Baghdad Observer* was handsome in its coverage of the British minister. The *Baghdad Observer* – no relation to the world's oldest Sunday newspaper – is an English-language newspaper which carries Saddam's version of world events. Most days – every day – it carries a photograph of Saddam. Yet although it serves Saddam's purposes, the *Baghdad Observer* contains all sorts of fascinating information. In particular, it is a great joy for the diligent student of Anglo-Iraqi friendship and co-operation. Courtesy visits by British ministers to Saddam which, for curious reasons, did not get a great play in the British media appear in enlightening detail in the *Baghdad Observer*. Its back issues are not secret, but freely available to members of the public who wish to pay the tube fare to Colindale in north London, and then cross the road to enter an ugly squat concrete utility building which houses the National Newspaper Library. Within lies a treasure house of sometimes embarrassing facts.

Take the issue of the *Baghdad Observer* dated Thursday 25 February 1988. The front page is dominated by a photograph of a patterned sofa. On the sofa sit two men: the President of Iraq and another, who is smiling brightly. The other is David Mellor, later to become the government's short-lived minister of fun. The *Baghdad Observer* reported: 'President Hussein asked the British minister to convey his greetings to Mrs Thatcher and Iraq's wish to develop friendship and co-operation with Britain on the basis of mutual respect and joint action to promote peace, security and stability in the region.'

How was Saddam? A series of calls was made to Mellor's office, about this and another subsequent and less well-known visit, as we shall see. But the former minister was too busy to talk.

Chatting with Saddam made some more than a little uneasy. Stephen Egerton was the British ambassador to Iraq from 1980 to 1982. He said: 'I'll tell you a story about Saddam Hussein. We went to a festival in the north. I took my family and my son said to me: "Daddy, can I see the great leader?" I said: "All right, we'll see if we can get near him." We managed by pushing and shoving to get near him and I said to him in Arabic: "Sir, this boy, my son, wants to meet you because he was born in Baghdad fifteen years ago." And Saddam said, quick as a flash:

"Ah, he's a tall boy, ask him when he's going to do his national service against the Kurds?" My son was absolutely horrified. I said to him: "That'll teach you to ask me to introduce you to Saddam Hussein." But I thought it was very quick response, in a ghastly way, witty, do you know what I mean? That's the sort of man he is. A quick wit, always to your discomfiture. He gave a half smile. He was half serious, half joking. But the effect was chilling . . . A very evil man.'

Mellor did not give his impressions of Saddam to the British newspapers, but he did express his thanks for the President's gracious act in releasing Smith: 'I believe the President granted clemency because of the improved relationship between Britain and Iraq.'

However willingly one applauds Mellor's statesmanship in freeing the British businessman, there is one germ of unease. Higson, the former Iraq desk man in the Foreign Office, explained: 'Saddam always liked to have a captive. At the Foreign Office we called it the "constant hostage syndrome". I used the word hostage in the sense of "pawn", a piece on the chessboard, to hold or sacrifice or let go. When Saddam let Mellor take Smith home, he knew Ian Richter was still inside prison.' Richter had been arrested in 1986 and released in 1991. Higson continued: 'It meant that he always had a hold on us. Still does – there are two hostages in Iraq now.' (They are Michael Wainwright, a globe-pedalling cyclist who was arrested when he crossed northern Iraq on his travels and Paul Ride, a cook who crossed the border into Iraq from Kuwait by mistake or was, more likely, abducted by the Iraqis.)

So there is another way of reading Saddam's clemency. He was playing a hostage game, one that Mellor and Mrs Thatcher played along with too. The Thatcher government prided itself that it never stooped to negotiate with the Hezbollah Shia hostage-takers, who abducted Terry Waite, John McCarthy and the others in the Lebanon. Perhaps Hezbollah never asked for machine tools.

Mellor's success with Smith cast a little shade over the parliamentary trip. The day after the *Baghdad Observer* reported

Mellor meeting Saddam, the newspaper boasted, 'President Saddam Hussein receives British delegation', and gave great prominence on its front page to a photograph of the sofa, Saddam sitting on it chatting to Tony Marlow. It went on: 'Members of the British Parliamentary delegation were appreciative of the Iraqi people's determination to defend their country . . . The President gave thorough and frank replies to a host of questions asked by the members of the delegation' – presumably a discreet reference to Adley's request to see the steam engines.

Everybody important was happy. Mellor had some nice headlines. Saddam appeared to the world as a clement states-man. More, the Iranian enemy and his internal opposition could see on Iraqi television and in the newspapers that on two consecutive days Saddam was fêted. First by a British minister carrying a letter from the British prime minister, then by a group of British parliamentarians. Far from being an international pariah for using poison gas and torture, Saddam appeared a respected pillar of the international community. (True, the opposition in Iraq was not happy. Sherko Omar of London's Kurdish community told me: 'Of course it was depressing to see a minister from a democratic country like Britain shake the hand of a dictator like Saddam. It helped Saddam because people did not see him as he really was. It made him look respectable.' But the proposition at the opening of this paragraph is: 'Everybody important was happy.' The opposition to Saddam was not important.)

The Right Honourable Members were pretty happy too. Richard Page recalled: 'I was given a photograph album with a big photo of me shaking hands with Saddam. Also a box of fudge.' Robert Hicks recalled a big photograph album of the visit. Roger Moate remembered 'a brass jug and some sweets at the airport'. David Young recalled: 'A brass jug. It was a kind of thing I would get in a bazaar. The lid had fallen off by the time I got back home.' Nick Budgen said: 'Wherever we went we were given some gifts. Nothing of any significance. Nothing I treasure.' Bob Parry described the photograph album: 'Not too ornate. I've had better albums. It's white and gold with Arabic designs. Plastic cover. There are about twenty pictures, quite a few of me with Saddam Hussein.' Michael Brown was asked about presents from the Baathist regime. The end of the conversation with researcher Alice Pitman was transcribed as follows:

QUESTION: Were you given any gifts?
BROWN: Yes. Ghastly Turkish delight . . .
QUESTION: Some MPs mention being given a brass jug.
BROWN: Yes, I believe I got some rather tacky thing like that. I threw it in the dustbin.
QUESTION: Did you have any dealings with the British Embassy?
BROWN: Of course I did.
QUESTION: What did you discuss?
BROWN: I don't want to discuss what I discussed.

The conversation ended in mutual stupefaction.

On the way home there was a security alert at Saddam Hussein International Airport. The alarms clamoured until investigation showed that the metal detectors had picked up a manufacturer's plate off a 1910 vintage 4-6-0, a manufacturer's plate off an early 1950s 2-6-4 tank engine, a manufacturer's plate off a Cowan Sheldon crane and an absolutely enormous spanner.

The MPs flew back to London. They flew the flag – the Iraqi flag, that is – on board an Iraqi Airways jumbo. First class, naturally. On his return home Brown discovered his Turkish delight had 'leaked in my suitcase on the flight back'.

'Choo-choo! Choo-choo!'

On the day that the *Baghdad Observer* carried the photograph of Marlow meeting Saddam, when David Mellor was still in Iraq, Saddam's men launched the poison gas offensive which killed 5000 Kurds.

The offensive started on the morning of Friday 26 February 1988. The Iraqis lost the battle, and withdrew from the Kurdish town of Halabja, near the border with Iran, retreating in the face of Kurdish guerrilla forces and the Iranian army. The Iraqis had their revenge on the town, full of unarmed and unprotected Kurdish civilians, on 16 March 1988.

At two o'clock in the afternoon a single warplane appeared from the west – the direction of Baghdad – and dropped one or more bombs, sending a thick yellow and white cloud through the town. Thousands of shells were lobbed into the town too.

The *Daily Telegraph*'s Norman Kirkham went to Halabja, with a gas mask, and reported what he saw on 22 March 1988. The *Telegraph* story was on page one. Kirkham's report read:

> Halabja has been left ruined and deserted – an open grave.
>
> Bodies lie in the dirt streets or sprawled in rooms and courtyards of the deserted villas, preserved at the moment of death in a modern Middle East version of the disaster which struck Pompeii.
>
> A father died in the dust trying to protect his child from the white clouds of cyanide vapour. A mother lies cradling her baby alongside a mini-bus which is slewed across the road, hit while trying to flee.
>
> Yards away a mother, father and daughter lie side by side. In a cellar a family lies crouched together.
>
> Shoes and clothes are scattered outside the houses. Carcases of cows lie still tethered to gateposts . . .

Nicholas Beeston in *The Times* also reported the scene on 22 March:

> Like figures unearthed in Pompeii, the victims of Halabja were killed so quickly that their corpses remained in suspended animation.
>
> There was the plump baby whose face, frozen in a scream, stuck out from under the protective arm of a man, away from the open door of a house that he never reached.
>
> Near by a family of five who had been sitting in their garden eating lunch were cut down – the killer gas not even sparing

the family cat or the birds in the tree, which littered the well-kept lawn.

Their neighbours had had the foresight to hide in an underground shelter. It became their mass grave with 10 men, women and children huddled together in the darkness, surrounded by their best carpets and the family's valuables . . .

Mrs Jamila Abdullah, aged 18, a teacher in Halabja's primary school, said: 'It was about half past six in the afternoon and the Iraqis had already left the town. I was at home when I heard the explosions and then smelt the bad smell.'

She had the presence of mind to douse her scarf with water and hold it to her face. But the other victims in the makeshift ward in the Iranian town of Bakhtaran, and those taken to Tehran for special treatment, were less fortunate. Nurses wearing black chadors went from bed to bed in the crowded Tehran clinic, administering cream to the twitching, contaminated limbs of the women and children, most of them writhing in agony . . .

Dr Said Foroutan [an Iranian expert on poison gas] . . . explained how the nerve gas and cyanide vapour killed their victims instantly, and how the sulphuric mustard gas left those it affected alive and in permanent agony.

The details were lost on one tearful Kurd [in Halabja], only one of 10 residents to be seen in the town, as he picked his way through the bloated carcasses of livestock and the bodies of his former neighbours.

'I do not know where my children are,' said Mr Abdul Rahman, aged 60 . . .

David Hirst in the *Guardian* reported the scene on 22 March:

No wounds, no blood, no traces of explosions can be found on the bodies – scores of men, women, children, livestock and pet animals – that litter the flat-topped dwellings and crude earthen streets in this remote and neglected Kurdish town in Iranian-occupied Iraq.

Its Arabic signs, not yet erased, offer 'Greetings, love and prosperity to the President-leader Saddam Hussein' and 'Death to the aggressors'.

The skin of the bodies is strangely discoloured, with their eyes open and staring where they have not disappeared into their sockets, a greyish slime oozing from their mouths and their fingers still grotesquely twisted.

Death seemingly caught them almost unawares in the midst of their household chores. They had just the strength, some of them, to make it to the doorways of their homes, only to collapse there or a few feet beyond. Here a mother seems to clasp her children in a last embrace, there an old man shields an infant from he cannot have known what . . .

Halabja was the worst documented case of a poison gas attack against civilians, ever.

The response of the British Foreign Office was well judged, given the need to balance the government's public distaste with its secret trade. The Iraqi ambassador to London, Dr Mohammed Sadiq al-Mashat, was called into the Foreign Office on 29 March 1988. He received an official protest from – who? The foreign secretary, Sir Geoffrey Howe? No. The minister of state for Middle-Eastern affairs, David Mellor, who was the guest of the Iraqis the day the gassing offensive started? No. The permanent secretary at the Foreign Office? No. The under-secretary at the Foreign Office? No. The deputy under-secretary of the Foreign Office? Yes. Dr al-Mashat was told by Alan Munro, whose diplomatic rank was virtually the most junior appropriate to conversing with an ambassador, that the British government was 'shocked' by the reports. According to the *Daily Telegraph* on 30 March 1988, Munro added that the government was distressed at the 'gruesome' pictures appearing in the media.

In the House of Commons on 30 March 1988, Sir Geoffrey Howe said: 'We have repeatedly made clear our condemnation of them [chemical weapons] and made representations specifically to the Iraqis.' On the same day Labour MP Jeremy Corbyn asked Mellor: 'Does the minister agree, however, that although he is right to condemn the use of chemical weapons against the Kurdish people in Iraq, one problem has been that the British government have maintained diplomatic relations with both Iran and Iraq, and not very long ago extended a £200 million credit to the government of Iraq, enabling them to prop up their economy and continue the prosecution of the war? Would it not be better if we withdraw all trade, aid and credits to both Iran and Iraq as a way of bringing to an end the war and the use of chemical weapons in the region?'

Mellor's reply is a model of Whitehall economy. He said: 'I think that would be an entirely self-defeating exercise. The fact that we have diplomatic relations with Iraq, for example, has made possible a wide range of contacts, to the mutual benefit of both countries, and enabled us to play a constructive part in the efforts of the United Nations to try to bring the Gulf War to an end. As recently as yesterday, it enabled a deputy under-secretary at the Foreign Office to see the Iraqi ambassador, to protest in strong terms about the use of chemical weapons, and to ask that his protest be reported back at the highest level in Baghdad. Without diplomatic relations, such exchanges would be impossible . . .'

Mellor answers Corbyn's point on the wisdom of diplomatic relations with Iraq, but regarding trade credits he leaves the MP treading on a step that isn't there. But the minister made a significant admission to his Labour shadow, George Robertson, in the same debate: 'It now seems clear that chemical weapons were used by Iraq against its own Kurdish population and the Iranian invaders. That use was contrary to international obliga-tions entered into by Iraq . . .'

The Iraqis took Britain and the West at their carefully modulated word. On 2 April 1988 the *Daily Telegraph* reported, '64 die in new Iraqi gas attack.' This time, Saddam's men had used poison gas against the Kurdish town of Karadagh. As a result of the Kurdish insurrection against Saddam, damning documentary evidence was seized by the Kurdish 'Peshmerga' – it means 'Those Who Face Death' – guerrillas of Iraq's poison gas arsenal. Helga Graham in the *Observer*, 27 March 1988, reported on the contents of two official documents which the Iraqi military had issued during its long and bitter campaign against Kurdish resistance.

The first is a letter from the Iraqi artillery command. It is headed, ironically, 'In the name of God, the Compassionate, the Merciful' and dated 3 August 1986. The letter was sent by General De'ah Abdul Waham Ezzat of Arbil district in Kurdistan to all units of the 24th Battalion. The subject, printed at the top of the letter, is 'Control over distribution of biological and chemical weapons'. Referring to a series of letters, all 'personal and highly confidential' from the Interior Ministry, the Defence Ministry, the special bureau of the Army Chief of Staff and National Defence Forces, the commander requires a half-yearly stock-taking of all chemical and biological weapons 'at the disposal of the units'.

The second is a telegram, dated 22 June but no year given and marked 'urgent and secret'. The telegram is from Major Sa'di Mahmoud Hussein, Commander of the Zakho District of Kurdistan to Commander 'A'. The purpose is to inform him that the KDP (Kurdish Democratic Party) have acquired 4000 gas masks. 'Saboteurs [i.e. guerrillas] will wear them when we use chemical weapons to attack their concentrations.'

There were more documents, including the text of a decree issued on 22 June 1987 by Ali Hassan al-Majid, the military governor of northern Iraq, known to the Kurds as 'Chemical Ali'. Note the echoes of Nazi diktats against the Jews contained in the document.

(1) All security-prohibited villages shall be considered to be bases of Iranian subversives and/or Iraqi traitors.

(2) Human and animal existence in these areas shall absolutely be prohibited and the areas shall be considered as operation zones in which shooting shall not be restricted by any instructions unless issued from our base . . .

(5) Anyone found within those prohibited areas shall be detained and interrogated by the security organs. Those whose

age lies between 15 and 70 years shall be executed after we
have benefited from their information . . .

I rehearse this evidence because it shows the extent of
knowledge about the Iraqi poison gas arsenal and its use against
the Kurds in the spring of 1988. At the time, unconfirmed stories
were circulating that the Iranians had also used cyanide gas
against the Kurds, but no serious evidence has ever been brought
forward to back this assertion. No legitimate Kurdish group has
ever complained that the Iranians used poison gas against them
– and in the past the Kurds have always complained about the
Iranians when they felt justified in doing so. In his book *Instant
Empire* Simon Henderson repeats the assertion that the Iranians
gassed the Kurds at Halabja, quoting an unnamed diplomatic
source and unnamed 'foreign military observers'. Blaming the
Iranians does, of course, serve the interests of Saddam and those
who wished to continue selling him arms unmolested. It also
appealed to some within the British Foreign Office and some
within the US State Department, who were so obsessed with the
menace posed to the West by the Islamic Republic of Iran that
they could not bring themselves ever to consider the Iranians in
the right. While it is not impossible that the Iranians gassed the
Kurds, it goes against all the available evidence: that the
Ayatollah personally had issued an order against Iran's use of
poison gas; that Saddam had announced he had decided to
punish the town for the 'crime of collaboration'; that Halabja
had been taken by the coalition of Kurds and Iranian forces; that
the alleged Iranian double-cross took place without any Kurds
suspecting it; that United Nations investigators in 1984, 1985,
1986, 1987 and three times in 1988 found the Iraqis to be the
guilty party on poison gas, despite systematic Iraqi attempts to
frame the Iranians (United Nations Security Council Report, S/
20134, dated 19 August 1988). Until those who make this
assertion emerge from their anonymity and provide evidence
which can be checked, one has to consider it with less weight
than one would a rumour from a carpet salesman in the Baghdad
bazaar – that being one likely source for the rumour if Hender-

son's 'foreign military observers' were Western military attachés in Baghdad. If, astonishingly, they were in Halabja, that is, on the front line, at the time of the attack and saw everything, where is their evidence? The most likely source for the rumour is, of course, the Amn or Mukhabarat or Estikhbarat or any other of Saddam's secret police forces, whose agents will have served their master well by muddying the waters at least as to Iraq's sole responsibility.

The document that nails Saddam on poison gas was held back from the United Nations for as long as possible: truth once more a victim of Saddam's lie machine. On 29 July 1988, Leonard Doyle of the *Independent* wrote that 'A damning UN report which concludes that Iraq has dramatically increased its chemical bombardments of Iranian civilian and military targets in recent weeks has been suppressed because of Iraqi influence on the Arabic translation service of the United Nations.'

Doyle reported that Iraqi interference had led to an inordinate delay in having the document translated into Arabic, blocking its simultaneous release in all six official UN languages. Once published, the report by Lieutenant-General Manuel Dominguez of the Spanish Army Medical Corps and Erik Dahlgren, a chemist of the Swedish Defence Research Institute, stated that Iraq 'is using chemical weapons more than ever before'. Despite the UN team being shown 'evidence' in Iraq of nine Iraqi soldiers who had been affected by chemical agents, the report did not conclude that Iran was using chemical weapons. The obvious implication of that non-finding was that the Iraqi casualties were 'own goals' – the result of poison gas clouds being blown back over their own lines or poorly targeted artillery shells and aerial bombardments. That is, in non-diplomatic language, the Iraqis had been lying.

Halabja marks a line in blood in our story. Up to the time in late March 1988 when the news of the Halabja gassing splashed on the front pages, it is perhaps possible to argue that the heaps of dead and mutilated victims of torture in Baathist Iraq were the result, as Neville Chamberlain said in a not very different context, 'of a quarrel in a far-away country between people of whom we know nothing'. Saddam had used poison gas against the Iranians and the Kurds in every year since 1983. He had bulldozed dozens of Kurdish towns and used chemical weapons in 1987. The international community had let those evils ride. But after Halabja, every businessman, minister and civil servant who visited or sanctioned further trade with Iraq has no excuse for not being aware of the nature of the regime.

Saddam's use of poison gas against the Kurds in the north and against their own troops in the south made the Iranians give up on the war. The Iranians were not above using Halabja for their own propaganda purposes, but television footage of the gassed civilians of Halabja had the reverse effect. Far from pressing on to Baghdad, Iranian troops started to retreat, frightened of and sickened by a war leader who would use poison gas against babies. Revolted though they were by the thought that Saddam might survive a war he started, the Iranian leadership grew despondent. Worse, Iraq embarked on a new phase in the 'War of the Cities', in March and April landing 200 missiles on Tehran. Iraq's modified Soviet Scud missiles could now reach the Iranian capital with their 412-mile range and 1200-pound warheads. Some of Saddam's missiles were exploded above ground, sending the obvious message that Iraq could deliver poison gas to the Iranian capital should it wish to. On a number of fronts, Saddam's forces pressed home their advantage, winning ground. The Ayatollah Khomeini is reported to have said that making peace with Saddam was as bitter as drinking 'a cup of poison'. But in August 1988, the eight-year war came to a halt.

War over, Saddam turned again on the Kurds. Words written here cannot do justice to what happened; the compression necessary in a book of this sort is unsatisfactory, even shameful, when set against the chronicle of agony. When confronted by the conflicting currents in human nature Martin Gilbert wrote in his awesome history *The Holocaust* (London: Collins, 1986), 'The historian is overwhelmed.'

Overwhelmed. And full of nausea. Those are the feelings one suffers when faced yet again by the scale of the evidence of

Saddam's barbarity: a small mountain of newspaper cuttings, detailing human misery on an epic scale; the frenzied appeal by Amnesty International to the United Nations Security Council – 'its first ever direct appeal' – 'to stop the massacre of Kurdish civilians by Iraqi forces'; the report of three eminent American doctors, members of Physicians for Human Rights; the explicit denunciations of the Iraqis' use of poison gas by the US State Department; even the stern denunciations by the British government – though there is, unhappily, something more to be added on that subject.

Take the first document to hand, sitting on top of the heap. It is from the Physicians for Human Rights, dated 22 October 1988, and headed 'Medical Team Finds Evidence of Iraqi Use of Chemical Weapons Against Kurds'. The team was led by Dr Robert Cook-Deagan, a research fellow at Georgetown University. The report states:

> Reliable testimony which confirmed the use of chemical weapons included:
>
> (1) bombing runs by low-flying jets were followed by the appearance of dark yellow clouds from the bomb-bursts;
>
> (2) death came suddenly to birds and domestic fowl, followed by sheep, goats, cows and mules ... The larger mammals were the last to die. Humans also died within minutes, without evidence of physical trauma;
>
> (3) refugees who had been within 75 to 300 metres of bomb-bursts described skin blistering which began within 30 minutes of exposure, and a characteristic pattern of severe irritation of the nose, mouth, skin and respiratory passages, nausea and/or vomiting, diarrhoea, headache, and painful urination ...

The full report carried the recollections of an eight-year-old girl, Aagiza:

> Soon after dawn on 25 August 1988, Aagiza saw planes suddenly appear over the mountain tops and unload bombs on Ekmala, her Kurdish village in northern Iraq. Seconds later,

the bombs exploded with a 'poof'. This was different from the loud explosions she and her family had grown accustomed to in previous attacks. A cloud of yellowish foul-smelling gas filled the air. Minutes later, she watched her parents and twenty-year-old brother die, and then she saw their skin blacken. Next, with other survivors, she undertook an arduous trip over high mountain passes into south-eastern Turkey. Her eyes and skin burned from caustic chemicals, she had difficulty breathing, and she had to stop occasionally to vomit. She coughed and had bloody diarrhoea. She refused to speak for four weeks . . . Her skin stung from blisters, which six weeks later are still healing. Aagiza now lives in a tent camp in Turkey . . .

Another witness for the doctors was a Kurd who lived in the village of Berjini:

It was about six in the morning when six airplanes showed up in the sky. They were turning around and two of them dropped some bombs which when they blasted had a very muffled sound . . . [High explosives might change the chemical composition of poison gas; to be dispersed effectively it requires a comparatively 'gentle' explosion – one of Wilfred Owen's poems refers, I think, to the 'soft crump' of gas shells.] . . . We were not used to that sound. After that, I looked around. I do not know how far it was, but I could see a cloud with a dark yellowish colour spread into the village. I could see that from far away the animals were dying, but I could not see anybody at that time standing up or walking around at the time the blast happened. But I could smell something garlic and my mouth became bitter and it became difficult to breathe. After the cloud disappeared, we went down and saw a lot of animals – birds, goats, sheep, cats, mules – were dead. And we saw a lot of people dead. I have their names. We counted fifteen people there: Hasanleh, Hasanaskenda, his son Kurdahasan, his other son Akinhasan, Salahsan, Hewhasan, Anyliamohamed, Disahamed, Mashimosh, Mohammed, Abdul Ahamed, Alymikal, Rumadommohamed, Afamismal, Rhisjoseph and

Asyrihasan. I knew all those people in the village and they were dead. When we looked at them, their skin was dark. They did not let us touch them. After that, we left the village. They said this is a chemical gas or poison gas. We left them behind and we went into the mountains to start the journey to Turkey.

Next in the heap are the press cuttings. David Hirst of the *Guardian* reported on 7 September 1988:

There are it seems only two words – gas and extermination – on the lips of the thousands of Kurdish refugees who had flooded across Iraq's northern border into Turkey in the past few days . . . 'Servass', a 28-year-old student, said: 'We did not imagine it could come on such a horrific scale. It was more widespread and brutal than Halabja. This is a war of extermination – the first time in history that gas has been used against civilians.' . . . The Peshmerga resistance said the Iraqis used artillery as well as aircraft, including crop-spraying planes, to deliver the chemicals. Two said that the Iraqis had adapted multiple rocket-launchers. The result, said one, was 'seas of gas' enveloping villages and valleys where civilians were hiding . . . 'We fear thousands are dead . . .' 'The crime the Iraqis have committed must reach the ears of the whole world . . .'

Paul O'Driscoll, writing in the *Observer*, reported on 11 September 1988:

At Cizre hospital in south-east Turkey, a group of doctors confirmed they had treated victims suffering from chemical burns. These patients were transferred to a better-equipped hospital at Mardin late last week. The doctors confirmed that their patients were suffering from blister burns to their hands and body and respiratory problems.

Marie Colvin of the *Sunday Times* reported, on 11 September 1988, that most of the seriously injured victims did not make it to Turkey across the mountains. One gas victim who did was Mohammed Hussein:

> ... who says he is 40 but looks 60 ... His face, hands, arms, and chest were a mottled white, studded with scabs, some of them still bloody. His forehead was edged with a dark, red-blue colour, and his ears were scabbed and swollen. He coughed phlegm and scratched his arms as he described the last stand at Lakh One, a large base in northern Iraq.
>
> 'We were 1000 fighting about 2000 Iraqi soldiers when suddenly I was enveloped in a white cloud. I don't know how it arrived. There was the smell of apples and I lost consciousness. There were bodies everywhere. I can't remember any more. It felt like the meat and muscle were coming off my bones, my eyeballs ached. My whole body still aches.'

There is more, all grisly. In the heap by my word processor lie batches of press cuttings, reports and eyewitness accounts which there is not enough space to rehearse here.

Forensic evidence of the Iraqis' use of poison gas was obviously difficult and dangerous to come by. But the Pentagon's Cold War listening technology had been tuned in to Iraqi military communications ever since May 1987 when an Iraqi warplane flying over the Gulf fired two missiles at the US frigate *Stark*, killing thirty-seven members of the ship's crew. The *International Herald Tribune* reported on 16 September 1988:

> Reagan administration officials say the United States intercepted Iraqi military communications indicating that Iraq had used poison gas against Kurdish guerrillas. The officials said the communications by the Iraqi Air Force were one source of evidence for US assertions that Iraq had used chemical weapons against the Kurds.

US intercepts of Iraqi military communications were almost certainly the source for the US State Department spokesman Charles Redman, who told reporters on 8 September 1988: 'As a result of our evaluation of the situation, the United States government is convinced that Iraq has used chemical weapons in its military campaign against Kurdish guerrillas ... We condemn this use of chemical weapons [and] we have expressed our strong concern to the Iraqi government.' Redman called the use of poison gas 'abhorrent'.

A few days later secretary of state George Schultz said that he was 'quite confident' that Iraq had used chemical weapons in its efforts to put down a rebellion by the Kurds.

And forensic evidence did become available, thanks to the efforts of British television film maker Gwynne Roberts, who was smuggled into northern Iraq by Kurdish guerrillas and returned to London with soil samples. (*See also* page 101.)

Let us take stock of the evidence thus far: in late August and early September 1988 more than 100,000 crossed the mountains from northern Iraq into south-eastern Turkey, some of them still marked by poison gas burns. More than 100,000 Kurds, eminent doctors, international journalists and the American secretary of state Schultz all agree that Saddam used gas against the Kurds. Set against that body of evidence are two, not wholly unrelated voices: the Iraqis and the British government.

In defence of the Iraqis, their denials were at least entirely predictable. The British ambassador in London, Mohammed al-Mashat denied the charges to anyone concerned. To express the disgust of the 'civilized world', in the words of the 1925 Geneva Accord, the British Foreign Office delegated – yes – deputy under-secretary Alan Munro to give al-Mashat a ticking off on 6 September 1988. However, the Iraqi line was not held with great conviction. Back in Baghdad, the Iraqi minister of defence, General Adnan Khairallah, edged around the question in a rare press conference. Clyde Haberman of the *New York Times* reported on 16 September 1988: 'While the Iraqi government in recent days has flatly denied the poison gas charges, Mr Khairallah was less than unequivocal ... Twice, for example, he said that he could give "a simple yes or no" about chemical warfare, but then declined to do so . . .' Khairallah even had a joke to tell about the gassings: ' "I was attracted by the fact that you haven't brought gas masks with you," he said. "If I were you, I'd have brought a mask, given the pictures drawn by the mass media."'

If the general had brought his gas mask along, it would probably have borne the proud boast: 'Made in Britain'. On 20 January 1991, the *Observer* reported that in 1983 Iraq bought 10,000 British-made NBC 'Noddy' suits. If the suits had been delivered promptly, the Iraqis could have used them in time for their first, experimental use of poison gas against Iranian troops in late 1983.

Iraq's cocktail of poison gas dropped on Halabja – a brew of hydrogen cyanide, tabun, sarin and sulphuric mustard gas – is thought to have been manufactured at the Muthanna gasworks near the town of Samarra. According to a report in the *Independent on Sunday*, dated 4 August 1991, the Muthanna gasworks was investigated by a United Nations team in June 1991. The newspaper reported a summary of the UN inspectors' findings. The site was

> huge, 25 square kilometres. Outside the United States and the Soviet Union, it is probably the third largest of its kind in the world. The inspectors were told it could produce 2.5 tons of the nerve gas sarin and five tons of mustard gas per day – ten times more than had previously been estimated . . . Among them [chemical weapons] are 30 nerve-gas-tipped Scud missiles . . . capable of reaching Israel.

The hydrogen cyanide used at Halabja was a close relation of the Zyklon B used by the Nazis against the Jews.

The UN, doubtless acting under pressure from Western governments, has thus far refused to disclose the precise details of the Western firms whose equipment was found in Iraq's various chemical weapons facilities like Muthanna.

British firms that inadvertently helped the poison gas programme included Nash Engineering, of Winsford, Cheshire, which supplied a sophisticated chlorine compressor to what it thought was a water purification plant in 1986. But chlorine is, of course, a major feedstock for poison gas. The *Daily Telegraph* reported a spokesman for the firm on 7 August 1991, who 'hoped to God' the plant was now 'in bits all over the desert' following Allied bombing of Iraqi chemical facilities. The export of the compressor was approved by the DTI and part-insured by the government's Export Credits Guarantee Department.

According to a report in the *Financial Times*, 22 November 1991, in its evidence to the Trade and Industry Select Committee, the government admitted that 'Customs and Excise is unable to find records of the supposed end-user of a 48,000 kg consignment of sodium sulphide sent in January 1988 – before the chemical was added to the warning list.' This admission came after the summer 1991 muddle when the DTI volunteered that it had allowed the export of known precursors of poison gas, then retracted that information amid massive confusion. Sodium sulphide is a known precursor of poison gas, but had been omitted from the DTI's watch list in error. Sodium sulphide and sodium cyanide were added to the warning list in May 1989, the *FT* reported. The newspaper added that almost three tonnes of two drugs that could be used as nerve gas antidotes were shipped to Iraq in April 1989. The government also conceded that the Customs and Excise microfilm records were not retained, and the only available information on British exports which might have helped Saddam gas the Kurds was available from February 1988 onwards, the paper reported. The answer to the question 'Did British technology help Saddam gas the Kurds?' is, as Dr Alastair Hay noted, 'We simply don't know.'

The late John Merritt, the *Observer*'s distinguished chief reporter, reported on 4 August 1991: 'Poisons for Iraq shipped via UK.' He quoted a senior Foreign Office source, who said: 'It seems that some of these substances [precursors for poison gas] were not actually made in Britain, but it was easier for the trade to come through here because of our more favoured trading status with Iraq. In that sense, we were a clearing house.'

However, it would not be true to say that the British government did not stop some chemical warfare-related exports. On 26 April 1988, the *Independent* carried the following headline:

'Export rules block aid to victims of gas attack.' Tom Wilkie reported:

> Export restrictions have prevented a group of scientists and doctors sending humanitarian and medical aid to Kurdish civilians attacked with poison gas during the Gulf War between Iran and Iraq.
>
> The group, the working Party on Chemical and Biological Weapons, was trying to send Kurdish doctors defensive equipment to protect civilians in any future attack . . . according to the group their attempts to buy equipment have been rebuffed by companies acting on instructions from the Ministry of Defence . . . A spokesman for Remploy, which makes decontamination kits, said: 'We have strict instructions, and there are certain countries to which we are not permitted to export NBC equipment.' Detectors to identify which type of gas was being used in any future attack were also restricted.

So the evidence – that which has not disappeared – shows that the British government permitted the sale of known precursors to poison gas to Iraq; of NBC suits to Iraq; of anti-nerve gas agents to Iraq. But it refused exports to the Kurds which might have helped them protect themselves against Saddam's poison gas.

In October 1988, a powerful indictment of the West's refusal to do anything serious about the Iraqi use of poison gas against its own people came in the shape of a US Senate report. Its authors, Peter Galbraith and Christopher Van Hollen, had been sent to Turkey by the chairman of the US Senate Foreign Relations Committee, Clairborne Pell, to investigate. The authors found that Iraq was using chemical weapons to depopulate Kurdistan. They argued: 'The end result of this policy will be the destruction of the Kurdish identity, Kurdish culture, and a way of life that has endured for centuries.' But the authors singled out Western apathy as a key factor in allowing Saddam to use poison gas with impunity. The report argued:

The lack of international response has encouraged Iraq to make more extensive use of chemical weapons. [Saddam may not care much about international opinion, but] the Iraqis do understand more direct forms of pressure. As it seeks to rebuild after eight years of warfare, Iraq will be looking to Western loans, to Western commercial credits, and to Western technology. Sanctions that affected Iraq's ability to borrow or to import Western goods, including technology, could make the price of continued chemical weapons use and of continuing the slaughter in Iraqi Kurdistan unacceptably high. This is particularly true since Iraq's most recent use of chemical weapons is totally unrelated to the struggle for national survival against Iran.

In the wake of the staff report, the Senate passed the Prevention of Genocide Act of 1988. President Reagan opposed it and it never got on to the statute books.

Precisely the same double-talk happened on the other side of the Atlantic. In London, a sterner tone in semi-public was at last used with the Iraqis. One possible explanation for the Foreign Office's soft whisperings of dismay rather than something tougher to the Iraqis about the use of poison gas in the past might have been because the victims were, in the main, the soldiers of the Islamic Republic of Iran. That Saddam was using poison gas against his own people appeared, in the Whitehall view, qualitatively a worse crime.

On 22 September 1988, John Bulloch of the *Independent* reported the toughest British criticism of Iraq yet. He wrote:

The Foreign Secretary, Sir Geoffrey Howe, with the Minister of State, Mr William Waldegrave [who had taken over from David Mellor in the summer of 1988], had a 70-minute meeting with Mr Saddoun Hammadi, the Iraqi Deputy Foreign Minister. In words rarely used in British diplomacy they spoke of 'British revulsion' at the Iraqi actions, calling them 'barbaric'.

Fine words.

'British revulsion' at the 'barbaric' Iraqis? Just over a month later a British minister went to Baghdad to double our trade credits for Saddam. It was 'All aboard' for UK Ltd on the Baghdad gravy train.

'Choo-choo! Choo-choo!'

CHAPTER
FIVE

Twice?

Five times?

Ten times? Twenty times? Thirty times? Forty times? Fifty times? A hundred times?

A thousand times?

No, just less: nine hundred and seventy-one times. In the autumn of 1988 the British government gave just less than a thousand times more aid to Saddam than to the Kurdish refugees sheltering from the Baathist killers in Turkey and Iran. The figures are as follows: the British government gave £250,000 in relief assistance to the Turkish Red Crescent Society via the British Red Cross Society to help. The European Community also gave £250,000, £100,000 of that sum from Britain making a total British contribution to the Kurdish refugees who fled from poison gas of £350,000. At the same time the British government approved £340 million in trade credits to Iraq. (It might be argued that the humanitarian aid was a straight gift while the trade credits were merely government 'insurance' for British firms trading with Iraq. However, come the invasion of Kuwait, Saddam treated the credits as a gift.)

The two British ministers who carried out the £340 million betrayal of the Kurds in November 1988 were the bagman who delivered the trade credits to Baghdad in person and the Treasury minister who effectively signed the cheques. The bagman who went to Iraq was Anthony Newton, a new face at the

Department of Trade and Industry who is now leader of the House of Commons; the Treasury minister responsible for the Export Credits Guarantee Department (ECGD) was the chief secretary, John Major, now prime minister. Neither Newton nor Major has ever explained at length why they chose to express Britain's dismay at Iraq's breach of the Geneva Accord of 1925 in its use of poison gas by extending more trade credits to the tyranny.

They doubled Saddam's money. The figures are plain: in 1987 the British taxpayer advanced Saddam £175 million in medium term trade credits; in 1988 the British taxpayer advanced Saddam £340 million in medium term credits, plus short term credits valued at £48 million. Such was the extent of 'British revulsion' at Iraqi 'barbarities'.

If Ali Hassan al-Majid was nicknamed Chemical Ali by the Kurds, could anyone have been blamed if Newton had been dubbed Chemical Tony for his part in aiding the Baathist economy? Newton was a serving Cabinet minister when he touched down at Saddam Hussein International Airport on 4 November 1988. He was in Iraq to show the flag at the Baghdad international trade fair.

How was Baghdad? It was a harmless question to put to the minister and a series of telephone calls were made to Newton's office about his trip. The calls started on 14 December 1992. That afternoon his adviser, Ian Stewart, returned the call and asked for more information. He was told it was about Newton's trip to Iraq. On 17 December a further call was made to Newton's office and a message left on an answerphone. Newton's adviser phoned back. He said: 'Haven't yet secured an answer. I'll get back to you.' On 18 December, Newton's adviser said: 'Tony Newton feels he is not able to offer you anything. It was a few years ago now and his recollection is pretty dim.' The adviser added: 'He didn't meet Saddam Hussein, anyway. Best of luck with your endeavours.'

Dim though Newton's recollections of Baghdad may be, a previous Conservative trade minister's memory of his time in Iraq more than eleven years ago is still bright and sharp. Students of Anglo-Iraq trade will be grateful to the Right

Honourable John Biffen who went to Baghdad from 30 September to 5 October 1981. We met at his comfortable wood-panelled office in the House of Commons, decorated with a spoof postcard entitled 'Prevent Street Crime', showing Margaret Thatcher stealing a purse from a woman's handbag. He is a Tory, but not painfully so. He speaks beautiful English, crisp with a sprinkling of vinegar.

'Being a trade minister is rather like being a door-to-door salesman. You find yourself saying things like: "How are you off for aircraft?" and that sort of thing. I was always selling Hawk trainer jets to anybody I bumped into.

'I remember meeting the then trade minister [Hassan Ali Saleh]. He looked like a pretty rough machine politician.'

A touch of the Al Capones? I asked.

'More like the sergeant major of the coup. Thick and slightly menacing. He greeted me with a bear-hug. He then produced a watch which he gave me. It was a Swiss watch. Our ambassador leaned over and whispered: "While you're here, Minister, you'd better wear the thing."

'The whole of the face was consumed with a picture of Saddam Hussein wearing a red-check headcloth. The reason I don't wear it is the Saddam face dominates the watch so much it makes it rather difficult to tell the time. One had to tilt it at the light so that you could guess the time. A tedious consideration but . . .' He didn't finish the sentence as we had both started to giggle. 'I had to declare the watch at Customs. The Customs man looked at it and thought about it, then said: "Left to yourself, sir, I don't think you would have bought a Mickey Mouse watch like that, so on you go." I still have it, locked away in Shropshire.'

With a small explosion of laughter he recalled, along with other garish trinkets, another Iraqi timepiece he was given as a present: 'I got the most appalling large alarm clock also with a picture of Saddam Hussein on it. Again, the form is that you register these gifts with the Treasury, and if you want to keep them someone comes along and values it and you pay the Treasury. I purchased the watch and the alarm clock via the

Treasury because of their memorable vulgarity.' The thought of waking up in the morning to a ringing bell and his first sight being the face of Saddam Hussein was so awful that Biffen admitted he did not make personal use of his present.

How did he find Iraq?

'Iraq? There was a soldier on every street corner. It was obviously a military regime. There is a viciousness which must go with much of the desert. I didn't like not being able to stay at the embassy. I didn't like staying in the government guest house. I thought it was bound to be bugged. I didn't like the climate. I didn't like the food. Inside the [Trade and Industry] Department, Iraq was a much valued market, especially in the context of the closure of the Iranian market. Whitehall was doing its best to push trade, because it feels guilty about the decline of manufacturing industry. Iraq was a good customer then, they were paying cash. It was the war with Iran which drained his treasure . . . [The choice of the word 'treasure' is pure Biffen English.] I had no strong desire to go back.'

Although Newton's recollections of his much more recent visit in 1988 are dim, there is documentary evidence from his own department which catches something of that trip's flavour. A press release at the end of his visit issued by the DTI, dated 7 November, made no mention of British concerns about human rights, the gassing of the Kurds or any local difficulties that might get in the way of Anglo-Iraq trade. Rather, the press release gushes with enthusiasm about our Iraqi trading partners. It boasts:

Speaking at the conclusion of the UK/Iraq Joint Commission trade talks in Iraq Mr Newton pointed out that the new trade credits, supported by the ECGD, the UK's official export credit insurer, are almost double those for 1988 [announced in 1987].

'This substantial increase reflects the confidence of the British government in the long term strength of the Iraqi economy and the opportunities for an increased level of trade between our two countries following the ceasefire in the Gulf war . . .'

The press detailed Newton's admiration of the 'close co-operation between Iraqi and UK organizers' at the trade fair and his meetings with senior Baathist ministers, including trade minister Dr Mohammed Mehdi Saleh, first deputy prime minister Taha Yassin Ramadhan, oil minister Issam al-Chalabi, finance minister Omar Mukhailif and Brigadier Hussein Kamil Hassan al-Majid (a close cousin of Chemical Ali Hassan al-Majid). The press release states baldly that the brigadier is from the 'Ministry of Industry and Military Manufacturing'. Hussein Kamil's office is normally translated as the Ministry of Industry and Military Industrialization, but the key word, which the DTI civil servant got exactly right in the press release, was 'Military'.

The question arises: why would a British trade minister want to meet the Iraqi brigadier in charge of 'military manufacturing'?

Newton was asked about his meeting with Brigadier Hussein Kamil on BBC Radio Four's programme *The World This Weekend* on Sunday 15 November 1992, after the collapse of the Matrix Churchill trial. That Sunday a front-page story in the *Observer* had quoted the DTI press release and cast more light on his trip to Baghdad. The relevant exchanges between Newton and interviewer Nick Clark are worth giving uncut and at some length, because they give an insight into the fluency and confidence of British ministers on the subject of trade with Iraq after the gassing of 5000 Kurds at Halabja and the 1988 summer offensive. Or otherwise.

NICK CLARK: Now I must raise with you the fact that today your own name has been put into the pot by the *Observer*. It points out that as a member of the team of the Department of Trade and Industry in 1988 to 1989 you were involved in decisions, indeed you were involved in a trip to Iraq, to meet the minister of military manufacturing, as part of what looked like a concerted drive to sell arms to Iraq. What do you say about your own involvement in this?

TONY NEWTON: Well, I'm not sure of the basis on which the *Observer* – I think it is, isn't it? – has made these [allegations], I suppose, their implicit allegation in its report today, and I must also say that I haven't had any opportunity whatever to check the papers that I would have been given in connection with that visit to Baghdad. But I can give you my very clear recollection which is that the basis of the visit was in connection with the possibility of us taking part in the civil, and I underline civil, reconstruction of Iraq following the damage that had been done during the war. The things that I had in mind were, for example, the pressures that we were getting from northern England to make sure that if generating capacity was needed, for example, in connection with power stations, that Britain shouldn't simply leave the business to the French and Germans and Italians. I remember a lot of talk about water supply and about pharmaceuticals. Nothing to do with arms exports. I do recall meeting a minister who as I recall was armed and my main recollection of the conversation was the sense of threat I felt when I started to protest about the use of chemical warfare.

CLARK: Now this may well have been Brigadier Hussein Kamil who was the minister of military manufacturing. Did you meet him? Do you recollect meeting him?

NEWTON: I would have to check, frankly, precisely which ministers I met. I do recall meeting two ministers who were armed and I do recall meeting the minister for trade but you must understand that I simply have not had an opportunity to look back at the arrangements that were made for something that occurred now, four years ago.

CLARK: But, of course, very soon after that was the Baghdad international exhibition for military production at which a lot of British firms were advertising goods which clearly were for military use. You must have been aware of what the British government's attitude was to these affairs?

NEWTON: The British government's attitude to these affairs which has been made clear on a number of occasions was that we were not exporting arms. Our policy was not to export arms-related equipment to Iraq or for that matter to Iran.

CLARK: And you're happy to stick by that despite all the evidence that's come out since?

NEWTON: What I'm saying is that I think the British government has adopted the appropriate course. We're getting and we've had more in the course of this programme endless allegations and innuendoes about whole ranges of individuals. I think that the right course is to have all that properly, thoroughly, independently, judicially investigated by Lord Justice Scott which is the process we've had in hand. But if you're asking me specifically whether I went to Iraq on any other basis than on an understanding that we were not, that our policy was not to export arms and arms-related equipment to Iraq, then that is the case.

A number of questions arise out of Newton's trip to Baghdad. First, why did the British trade minister meet the Iraqi minister 'for military manufacturing', according to the DTI's own press release boast in November 1988? Second, is Newton correct in telling the BBC that government policy was 'not to export arms and arms-related equipment to Iraq'? If that was the case, then all the arms-related equipment, such as encryption units, radios, army lorries, engine parts for fighter jets, which were licensed for export to Iraq were in contravention of government policy. Third, if Newton felt unease when he raised the question of chemical weapons with the Iraqis, why did he not cancel the trade credits to the tyranny there and then? Fourth, why did the trade minister and the then chief secretary John Major choose, in the wake of the evidence on Halabja and the summer offensive, to all but double those trade credits? Fifth, was he offered a Saddam Hussein Mickey Mouse-style watch as Biffen was? It was not possible to put these specific questions to Newton because of his general refusal through his adviser to 'help' with the question of his trip to Baghdad.

Newton may not make much of the trip today, but the *Baghdad Observer* gave his visit its usual puffs at the time. Having been knocked by a wave of international protests over its use of poison gas throughout 1988, the Baathist tyranny was happy to make as much political capital as possible out of the official British delegation.

During the course of his visit, the following headlines appeared in the *Baghdad Observer* featuring his presence: on 6 November 1988: 'Iraq, Britain discuss trade, economic ties' and 'Thousands visit Fair'; on 8 November 1988, 'Iraqi-British ties reviewed' and on 9 November 1988, 'Ties with . . . Britain discussed'.

As with the Mellor visit earlier in the year, the effect of such Cabinet level visits to Baghdad did little for the brutalized opposition in Iraq. Dr Dlawer Ala'Aldeen (the name is a slightly different transliteration of Aladdin – he of the lamp) is a Kurd, now working as a physician and research scientist in Nottingham University Hospital. He is an effective and thoughtful spokesman for Kurdish rights, who went on a tour of embassies in 1988 to highlight Saddam's serial atrocities. That tour was undermined when three Arab ambassadors, from Iraq, Kuwait and Saudi Arabia subsequently toured the same embassies, putting Saddam's case.

Asked about the contrast between Britain's openly stated repugnance of Saddam's use of poison gas and its trade minister having doubled trade credits and met Iraq's minister of 'military manufacturing', Dr Ala'Aldeen said: 'It couldn't be more depressing. Sometimes it could be called disgusting. Any visits would increase the respect he would enjoy in the international community.

'When we went to see them the British government was very nice to us. Their response was most sympathetic. They diffused the charge. Now we know at the same time they increased trade with Iraq. The British government was playing a double game.

The industrial lobby was much more important than the humanitarian lobby. When we saw British ministers shaking hands with the dirtiest hands of all . . .' His voice broke off in dismay. 'Whoever supports a regime like that must take some share of the blame. Whatever way you help the regime, you will help Saddam kill more people.'

Conclusive forensic evidence of Saddam's use of poison gas was broadcast in late November 1988. The proof was provided by independent film maker Gwynne Roberts who had dared to go into northern Iraq, guided by Peshmerga guerrillas, in September 1988. The Channel 4 *Despatches* programme 'Winds of Death' presented the viewers with ghastly eyewitness accounts of the gas-bombing of a trail packed with refugees on 28 August 1988. One interviewee, a Peshmerga guerrilla called Ramazan Mohammed, had watched the attack on the civilians, mainly women and children, from higher up the mountains. There was nothing the guerrillas could do. He said: 'There must have been 3000 bodies and thousands of animals, all dead. The dead had a film over their eyes. Out of their nose and from the sides of their mouth there was a horrible slime coming out. The skin was peeling and bubbling up.'

But Roberts's great achievement was to collect soil samples from a bomb-hole just inside Iraq at no little risk. The spot was ten miles west-south-west of the confluence of the frontiers of Iraq, Turkey and Iran. At the site, a large, thin-walled metal bomb was found embedded in the ground. The bomb had ruptured so soil was excavated from under it and placed in a brown, plastic screw-top jar. Two metal fragments from inside the bomb and a sample of what appeared to be sheep's wool were also recovered. On his return to England, the samples were sent to commercial chemical analysts in Birmingham, the firm of Clayton, Bostock, Hill and Rigby. The analysts found traces of two volatile breakdown products from mustard gas, 1,4-oxathiane and 1,4-dithiane, plus the explosive TNT. This hard scientific evidence was made available shortly before transmission of the *Despatches* programme and broadcast on 22 November 1988.

The hard evidence collected by Roberts and analysed in

Britain makes what happened next appear all the more astonishing. Foreign secretary Sir Geoffrey Howe stood up in the House of Commons on 30 November 1988, and spoke not for England but for Iraq. He combined the usual platitudes expressing distaste at the displacement of the Kurds with a significant retreat on Iraq's proven use of chemical weapons, allowing the Iraqis off the hook. Sir Geoffrey noted the results of the *Despatches* programme, but told the House: 'We have certainly been appalled by the suffering inflicted as a result of the large-scale displacement of Kurds from their homes in Iraq. We have proclaimed the evidence of CW use as compelling but not conclusive.'

But not conclusive – three words which provided great succour to Iraq. The 100,000 refugees fleeing 'seas of gas', the American doctors, the international journalists, the serial United Nations reports, his own previous junior minister, David Mellor, who admitted that poison gas had been used at Halabja, the Pentagon's billion-dollar listening technology and Clayton, Bostock, Hill and Rigby had all got it wrong. Or, at least, had failed to prove Iraq's guilt to the British government.

But not conclusive – three words which provided a formula for the doubling of trade credits to Iraq, authorized by Chief Secretary Major and handed over by Trade Minister Newton, to stand.

But not conclusive – three words which allowed Britain's secret arming of Iraq to accelerate into top gear.

Immediately after transmission, scientists at the United Kingdom Ministry of Defence's Chemical Defence Establishment at Porton Down got in touch with Gwynne Roberts and asked to re-analyse the samples. The scientists at Porton Down confirmed the programme's analysis and, even better, they found not just the breakdown products of mustard gas but traces of mustard gas itself: absolute proof of Iraq's breaking of the 1925 Geneva Accord. Porton Down stated that sample one, the soil taken from underneath the bomb, was 'relatively heavily contaminated with sulfur mustard [mustard gas] and related decomposition products or impurities'. They sent their research results – Reference

Number PTN/TG 1090/3/36/88 – to Roberts on 11 January 1989, but according to Dr Alastair Hay of Leeds University the government could have known the results of the Porton Down test within days of receipt of the samples. 'I have no doubt that Porton Down would have turned these samples round pretty smartly,' he said. The last two digits of the reference number suggest that the research was carried out in late 1988. An official from Porton Down confirmed on 23 December 1992 that the tests were carried out 'round about 14 December 1988'.

It is inconceivable that Porton Down did not report the results to Whitehall as soon as possible. Whitehall would have known that the tests were being carried out following transmission of 'Winds of Death' in late November; Porton Down had the results around 14 December 1988; they sent them on to Gwynne Roberts on 11 January 1989. But subsequent correspondents to government ministers, asking about Iraq's use of chemical weapons, were given the Howe 30 November 1988 'but not conclusive' formula which had been quickly overtaken by the results of the Porton Down tests. For example, William Waldegrave wrote on 19 January 1989, to John Bowis, MP, after a letter from one of his constituents, Mrs Gulay Yurdal-Michaels. Waldegrave included a lengthy background note with his reply. The note stated: 'There are also compelling indications that chemical weapons were used in August 1988. If so . . . the suspected use of CW . . .' All this and more, written as if document PTN/TG 1090/3/36/88 did not exist.

The government finally admitted that the evidence was 'convincing' on 31 January 1989, when the political heat had lowered. That day, the junior defence minister Archie Hamilton (another Old Etonian) informed the House of Commons in a written answer:

> The Chemical Defence Establishment Porton Down has carried out a scientific analysis of soil samples provided by Mr Gwynne Roberts, a Channel 4 reporter. The analysis, which was given to Mr Roberts on 11 January [this wording also suggests Whitehall knew the results of the Porton Down tests

some time before they communicated with Roberts], shows
that samples contained traces of sulphur mustard and related
compounds together with traces of the explosive Tetryl [TNT].
We cannot confirm the circumstances in which these samples
were collected, but have no reason to doubt Mr Roberts's
account that these were collected in northern Iraq. The
Government believe that this, following previous indications,
amounts to convincing evidence that chemical weapons have
been used by Iraq against their Kurdish population.

But Hamilton had failed to pass on the good news to Lord
Trefgarne, minister of state for defence procurement. Trefgarne
danced round the question of Iraq's use of poison gas – on the
very same day as Hamilton's written answer to the Commons –
during a debate on chemical weapons in the House of Lords.
You may care to savour Lord Trefgarne's debating skills. There
follows almost the Platonic ideal of Whitehall economy with the
truth.

LORD CLEDWYN OF PENRHOS: Does he not agree that the case
of using chemical weapons was proven beyond doubt against
Iraq in relation to the recent war with Iran and in relation
to the Kurds?

LORD TREFGARNE: My Lords ... I must agree that there is
powerful circumstantial evidence to support them. However,
they are denied by the country concerned [Iraq] ...

LORD GRIMOND: My Lords, in the case of Iraq, is it not true
that casualties who were clearly identified as suffering from
the effects of chemical weapons were examined by impartial
doctors from other countries and that the charges were
proved to the hilt?

LORD TREFGARNE: My Lords, it is the case that we saw some
[sic] casualties from Iraq who, it was alleged, were suffering
from the effects of chemical weapons. It is very difficult to be
certain in such cases; nevertheless, as I said in answer to the
noble Lord, Lord Cledwyn, the circumstantial evidence was
considerable.

BARONESS SEEAR: My Lords, can the noble Lord tell us what evidence there is, contrary to the evidence of the doctors, that it was not chemical weapons which were used against these people?

LORD TREFGARNE: My Lords, as I recall it, there was no doubt about the cause of the injuries concerned; namely, the presence of certain chemicals. However, whether those chemicals came to those people in contravention of the 1925 protocol is another matter ... The 1925 protocol ... provides only for the prohibition of the use of chemical weapons between contracting parties to the protocol. It is not clear that that is what happened in this case. For example, I am not entirely certain that the Kurds were contracting parties to the protocol ...

One can summarize the noble Lord's positon: 'Heads – they weren't gassed; tails – gassing doesn't count.'

Thanks to the documents prised out of Whitehall by the Matrix Churchill defence, we can see Sir Geoffrey's and Lord Trefgarne's astonishing refusal to accept the overwhelming case against Iraq on poison gas in a wider context.

A further refinement of the art of telling the truth.

On the same day that Newton set off for Iraq, 4 November 1988, his junior colleague at the DTI, Alan Clark, wrote to William Waldegrave at the Foreign Office. Clark urged a policy of 'relaxing control on a growing number of categories as peace takes hold', arguing that export licences for spare parts for civil aircraft and helicopters, communications and transport equipment and machine tools should all be granted by ministers. Clark made two references to documents that have yet to see the light of day, a note from Sir Geoffrey Howe, dated 31 August, and a letter from Number 10 Downing Street. Clark wrote: 'I recognize, of course, that whatever is agreed between us will require the Prime Minister's approval in the light of her Private Secretary's letter of 2 September.'

One can therefore deduce that both the then foreign secretary and the prime minister had taken an active interest in the problems created by trade with Iraq; and that these documents had been weeded from the sequence of minutes and correspondence handed over to the defence.

There is no mention of any problems about trading with Iraq because of its use of poison gas against the Kurds. There is, however, a note that the government might face 'presentational' difficulties. Clark wrote: 'I would not propose an announcement of any decision to issue the outstanding licences but we should be prepared to explain our decision if necessary and appropriate defensive briefing would need to be available to meet possible criticism.' He added that he would be copying this letter to the prime minister and Lord Trefgarne, the minister of state for defence procurement. Clark ended his letter by adding in his own hand: 'This is important.'

As well as pushing through export licences which had been delayed because of the guidelines, Clark and his civil servants at the DTI were also campaigning for the scrapping of or, at least, looking again at the Howe guidelines. By the end of 1988, they resembled a mouldy chunk of Gruyère – that is the cheese which comes ready-made shot full of holes. For example, the Matrix Churchill documents show that civil servants referred up to ministers the prickly question of whether two Browning 9-mm pistols should be allowed to go to Iraq. A note of the Interdepartmental Committee (IDC) – a meeting of civil servants from the DTI, MOD and the Foreign Office – on 24 February 1988, recorded:

> The IDC agreed that this equipment was clearly lethal and therefore prohibited under our embargo on lethal weaponry. However, MOD informed the IDC that, because the consignee was Saddam Hussein's son [believed to be Uday Hussein, also a murderer] they intended to draw this application to the attention of ministers.

The trial documents give no further clue to the outcome, but pearl-handled pistols, rifles and shotguns were included in a list of exports approved by the DTI in 1988 and 1989. Although small in number, pistols, rifles and shotguns are lethal weapons. That they were licensed for export to Iraq shows that the Howe guidelines were breached and that ministers, in this respect at least, misled the House of Commons when they declared that Britain did not export arms to Iraq.

The first inkling that the guidelines were to be softened came on 2 August 1988, when the United Nations report on Iraq's use of poison gas was at last being published in New York. A paper from the IDC on that date listed applications that might be affected by a 'gradual relaxation' of the guidelines following a ceasefire or settlement of the Iran–Iraq conflict. At the next meeting of the IDC a Matrix Churchill application to sell lathes to Iraq was raised as a 'special case of a large order being held up by the delay in approval for the relaxed export guidelines'.

It was the pressure from British firms which put the DTI on the offensive. By early December 1988, the Gruyère was more holes than cheese. Consider the Foreign Office minutes of the IDC, dated 1 December 1988, which sidestepped the issues raised by an application to export sporting gun cartridges to Iraq by claiming that they fell outside the guidelines 'particularly now that the Secretary of State [Howe] had spoken of a more flexible interpretation of the guidelines'. The IDC recommended approval.

Later that month the three ministers now at the heart of the Iraqgate affair – Alan Clark at the DTI, Lord Trefgarne at the Ministry of Defence and William Waldegrave, minister of state at the Foreign Office – agreed to change the Howe guidelines. The revision made the guidelines even more porous, but it represented a kind of victory for the Foreign Office over the DTI, who wanted them scrapped altogether. The significant change was to guideline three.

Sir Geoffrey Howe had announced in 1985: '(iii) We should not approve orders for any defence equipment which, in our view, would significantly enhance the capability of either side to prolong or exacerbate the conflict.'

This was changed to: '(iii) We should not in future approve orders for any defence equipment which, in our view, would be of direct and significant assistance to either country in the conduct of offensive operations in breach of the ceasefire.'

No one, of course, told Parliament. The rule change was kept secret. In April 1989, ministers decided on a form of words to be used in Parliament which was broad enough to cover the revision but would not indicate to MPs that anything had been changed. They also agreed on a secret tilt to Iraq. Waldegrave's private secretary wrote to Alan Clark in a letter on 27 April 1989:

> We agreed that we should continue to interpret the guidelines more flexibly in respect of Iraq, as we have done in practice since the end of last year; but that we should revert to a stricter interpretation for Iran, along the lines which operated before the ceasefire.

The document adds:

> It was preferable not to have to announce any change in them [the guidelines].

The form of words to be used if ministers were pushed on the issue in Parliament was:

> The guidelines on the export of defence equipment to Iran and Iraq are kept under constant review, and are applied in the light of prevailing circumstances, including the ceasefire and developments in the peace negotiations.

The formula worked. No one guessed that ministers would change the rulebook without letting Parliament know. By one of those sweet ironies that enrich this story, Waldegrave is now the minister responsible for open government.

So the view from Baghdad as 1988 turned into 1989 looked like this. Saddam had used poison gas against the Iranian enemy to terrify them to the peace table, and then he had used poison gas against his own people in Iraqi Kurdistan. The West, and the British Foreign Office in particular, had expressed their anger, but it was muted. Far stronger signals were made, giving Baghdad the green light. Britain had sent a parliamentary delegation who had paid their respects at the Iraqi Tomb of the Unknown Soldier. One British minister, David Mellor, had come to Iraq to praise Saddam's clemency in return for a British hostage. Another had come to Iraq to double the trade credits. A third announced that there was no conclusive proof that Saddam had been using poison gas after all. The Iraqis had two of their top spies, Habobi and Kadhum, in place in London, buying everything the country needed to build its superweapon arsenal. Baghdad could afford to shrug off the criticisms, and buy up the bits to make its first nuclear bomb – trade insured by the ever-generous British taxpayer.

CHAPTER
SIX

Immediately after the invasion of Kuwait the hunt for the Iraqi arms-buying network was on. The best and the brightest of British journalism were after Saddam's men. One of the most potentially interesting leads was the offices of TDG, the headquarters in Chiswick, west London, of Saddam's technobandits, the team led by the senor Iraqi military intelligence officer, Dr Safa Habobi, and the lawyer for the Iraqi ministry of industry and military industrialization (MIMI), Fadel Kadhum.

One night in August 1990 two journalists sat in one of the many milk bars in west London, thinking how they could find out what the Iraqis had been up to. The dustbins! Towards midnight an investigative journalist – who has asked not to be identified – and the late Paul Jenks, a brilliant and fearless freelance photographer, crept around the back of the Iraqis' offices. There were eighteen black bin bags, lined in a row. They delved through used tea bags, coffee filter papers, apple cores and a mountain of rubbish before, in the eighteenth bag, they struck gold: TDG paperwork, torn up but not shredded. They took the strips of paper home, sat down on the kitchen floor and matched up the jigsaw. In the small hours of the morning the realization dawned that on the kitchen floor lay documentary evidence that Habobi's team was using London as a base to buy into other European machine tools firms, part of Iraq's strategy to become a nuclear power. The evidence on the kitchen floor was subsequently passed on to the BBC's *Panorama*, which broadcast what was in the Iraqis' dustbins to a wider public.

The dustbin documents showed that TDG bought an 18 per cent stake in Schmiedemeccanica, a Swiss firm specializing in precision forging of high-tech components, with an intention to buy up more of its stock. The company told the world that the parts were for gear forgings, but German Customs believed the components were destined for Iraq's nuclear weapons programme and seized them at Frankfurt airport.

Whitehall's mandarins and their political masters did not have to poke around in Habobi's dustbins to discover that he was after nuclear technology in Britain and abroad. British intelligence knew before Christmas 1988 what Habobi was up to. On 23 December 1988, a minute marked 'Secret UK Eyes' said the intelligence service – it is not evident whether that means MI5 or MI6 – had identified the procurement network run by Habobi that 'had attempted to obtain gas centrifuge components from the UK'.

It is not clear from the Matrix Churchill documents who was the intelligence source for this new evidence of Iraq's nuclear ambitions. MI6 were thinking of reactivating Henderson, whom they had used when he had travelled frequently to the Soviet bloc some years before, but they had not done so by the turn of 1988/1989. MI6 renewed its contacts with Henderson formally on 24 April 1989.

Mark Gutteridge was still in regular touch with the roly-poly James Bond from MI5, though he had left Matrix Churchill in late 1988 for a job with another company. The spy known to the Old Bailey trial court as Ford reported to his analysts at MI5 on 12 December 1988. After 'an update on the Iraqi situation [two lines deleted] . . . (Details shown separately). We then left the hotel to collect Mrs Gutteridge to take supper in their favourite Italian restaurant.'

This was Portofino in Kenilworth, which rates a favourable if not gushing mention in the 1987 *Good Food Guide*: 'veal is well sauced and puddings on a par.'

The next two lines of Ford's 'Secret' report have been

deleted. Looking at the blacked-out words, one falls prey to the uneasy suspicion that the taxpayer may well have been footing the bill for Ford treating himself to the well-sauced veal. Equally, it may have been 'Gutteridge told me all about Habobi's nuclear ambitions.' The weeder's pen blots out all.

Whatever the origin, the 23 December 1988 secret intelligence was accurate. Foreign office minister William Waldegrave was informed of Habobi's nuclear shopping list in early February 1989. He had to decide whether the Foreign Office should approve or seek to stop three applications for Matrix Churchill lathes, worth £5.3 million, to be exported to Iraq. Should the Foreign Office let them go? In the context of that question, Stephen Lillie of the Foreign Office's Middle Eastern department minuted to Waldegrave on 1 February 1989:

> There has since been evidence [the following half line has been deleted – presumably this is a reference to a security source] which implicates another part of Habobi's procurement network (but not Matrix Churchill itself) [presumably TDG] in Iraqi attempts to obtain equipment for the development of gas centrifuge technology for uranium enrichment. This is a serious development which confirms our long-held suspicions that Iraq, although a party to the Treaty on the Non-proliferation of nuclear weapons (NPT), has ambitions to develop a nuclear weapons capability.

It was known by everybody who needed to know in Whitehall that British machine tools were making munitions in Iraq; that Saddam had used Western technology to manufacture poison gas which he had used abundantly; and now, in February 1989, it was evident that Saddam's London-based agents were working on his ambition to be a master of the first Arab nuclear power.

Lillie went on:

> There is good reason to be sceptical about allowing any export which might help in the achievement of Iraq's nuclear objec-

tives. However, officials from interested departments have agreed that there is no reason to believe that Matrix Churchill lathe equipment is of specific interest to the Iraqi nuclear programme . . .

After Lillie raised the nuclear fears on paper, he neatly glissaded away from them. Rather, he reminded Waldegrave of the potential loss of jobs and the potential loss of intelligence – which might provide further evidence on Iraq's nuclear ambitions – if the exports were not licensed. He recommended that all three applications be approved. He concluded his lengthy 1 February 1989 minute: 'It is doubtful that wider political considerations will have been sacrificed in favour of short-term commercial objectives.' With the benefit of hindsight, one could repeat Lilley's conclusion, only changing the word 'doubtful' for 'doubtless'.

Waldegrave faced some opposition from his fellow Old Etonian the Honourable David Gore-Booth, an Arabist in the Foreign Office who had done his stint at the Baghdad embassy in the sixties. Of all the officials in the saga, Gore-Booth appears thus far in the narrative to be the only one who expressed some reservations about trading with Saddam. However, he lost this round. Waldegrave scribbled in his spidery hand across the top of Lillie's minute: 'Yes, I agree. Screwdrivers are also required to make H-bombs.'

It was an arms-dealer's apologia of tea-towel-maxim banality. It was also dead wrong.

The UN nuclear inspectors charged with turning upside down Iraq's nuclear programme as part of the UN ceasefire from spring 1991 found Matrix Churchill machine tools inside the country's nuclear facilities. UN Security Council document Number S/23947, dated 22 May 1992, reported on the eleventh on-site inspection inside Iraq. On page 17 the inspectors said: 'The Iraqi side stated that the small components for the centrifuge prototypes were manufactured outside Iraq by three companies – C. Plath [of Germany], Schaublin [of Switzerland] and Matrix Churchill.' The import of this report should not be understated: the Iraqis claimed to the United Nations that the nuclear components had been made outside Iraq. This begs two questions: first, were the Iraqis telling the truth to the UN investigators, and, second, did the machine tools companies in Germany, Switzerland and Britain know what the 'small components' they were manufacturing were for?

After the collapse of the Matrix Churchill trial, more evidence appeared in the newspapers. One unnamed nuclear inspector told Steve Boggan of the *Independent*, 12 November 1992: 'I saw a Matrix Churchill CNC multi-axes milling machine at the Nassir Establishment for Mechanical Industries in Taji, where it was involved in the gas centrifuge programme.' Gas centrifuge technology is one route towards refining weapons-grade uranium.

The inspector (quoted in the *Independent*) continued:

> Matrix Churchill machinery was also at an engineering complex in Salahuddin that was used in the production of gas centrifuges, shells and armaments like sea mines. And at a manufacturing site in Badr, Matrix machinery was involved in the production of calutrons. [Another piece of atomic/nuclear bomb kit.] I don't know what the British laws are on exports, but if the British government was doing what I think it ought to have been doing, we shouldn't have found that equipment in Iraq.

The managing director of Matrix Churchill, Paul Henderson, has rebutted claims that his company knowingly had anything to do with making nuclear components. Henderson was quoted in an *Observer* article by Peter Beaumont and Alan George on 27 December 1992 stating that he had no 'personal knowledge' that his company had produced prototypes for Iraq's nuclear programme although he conceded that they 'could have been made' without his knowledge. He added: 'I am fairly confident that the Matrix Churchill factory never made any parts for centrifuges.' He said he 'wouldn't have a clue what a centrifuge part looked like'. (It is, of course, entirely possible that Matrix Churchill made small components without knowing they were for the Iraqi nuclear programme. The whole strategy of the Habobi arms network was to disguise from Western businesses their true aims.)

Some of the Foreign Office civil servants may have played down the impact of the news of the Habobi ring trying to buy nuclear technology in early 1989, but they did pass on the information to the political master, Waldegrave. What went wrong was that the minister chose to err on the side of not offending the Iraqis.

Waldegrave's support of British technology going to Iraq – even at the risk of helping its nuclear programme – was not academic. A few days after his 'screwdrivers' decision, on 13 February 1989, Waldegrave himself touched down at Saddam Hussein International Airport, to do his little bit for the further-ance of Anglo-Iraq relations. The Iraqis had the 'tousle-headed and Byronic' (Matthew Parris, *The Times*) Old Etonian for breakfast. That a Richard Waldegrave was a speaker to the House of Commons in the fourteenth century, that Sir Henry Waldegrave took the hand in marriage of James II's illegitimate daughter by Arabella Churchill in 1686, cut no ice with the Baathist regime. They may have smiled at his preferred pronun-ciation of his surname – 'Walled-grave' – but otherwise they gave not an inch.

Waldegrave's freedom to protest over Iraq's gassing of the Kurds – if he had been so minded – was greatly diminished because of the 'constant hostage syndrome'. Still rotting inside Baghdad's notorious Abu Ghraib prison was Ian Richter, then forty-three, a married man with three children and a British water engineer. He was arrested in June 1986, given a forty-five minute trial before a revolutionary court in February 1987, and sentenced to life imprisonment on a charge of bribing the mayor of Baghdad, who was later executed. There is no mention in the minutes that any minister or civil servant ever considered delaying exports or holding back trade credits as leverage against Saddam.

While in Baghdad Waldegrave did not gain an audience with Saddam, but he did see the Iraqi foreign minister, Tareq

Aziz. The Iran–Iraq ceasefire was discussed, as was the situation in the Gulf, the Arab-Israeli conflict, bilateral relations and trade. According to John Bulloch of the *Independent*, 14 February 1989:

> What was not mentioned was the Iraqi campaign against its own Kurdish population, and the regular use of chemical weapons by the Iraqi army during its drive against rebellious minorities in the north of the country ... Waldegrave had hoped to see him [Richter] freed as a gesture of Iraqi goodwill towards Britain. But the British minister was due to travel alone to Kuwait, and Iraqi officials held out no hope of an early pardon. Britain's tactful silence earned no reward.

Bulloch does not cite any evidence for his assertion that Waldegrave was silent about the gassing of the Kurds. It would be extraordinary if the minister had not rehearsed 'British revulsion' at the regime's 'barbaric' gassing, as he himself, with Sir Geoffrey Howe, had used those words with the Iraqis in London in September 1988. But, then again, Bulloch is a well-respected journalist with good contacts, and the still current Foreign Office line on Iraq's use of poison gas against the Kurds was that the evidence was 'not conclusive', as opposed to the two, contradictory lines from the MOD, namely that the evidence was 'convincing' (Hamilton) or 'circumstantial' (Trefgarne).

The *Baghdad Observer*, of course, milked the Waldegrave visit for every last drop of its propaganda yield. 'Iraq, Britain to enhance bilateral co-operation' it boasted in its stilted idiom. The body of the story concerned a meeting between Waldegrave, who had just sanctioned further exports by Matrix Churchill to Iraq, some of which ended up in the Iraqi nuclear programme, and the Baathist figure in command of that programme, Hussein Kamil Majid, the minister for industry and military industrialization and Saddam's son-in-law.

Trip over, Waldegrave's office wrote to Alan Clark at the DTI on 27 April 1988, emphasizing that Britain should 'continue to interpret the [Howe] guidelines more flexibly in respect of

Iraq', but that it was preferable not to announce publicly any change in them. Earlier in the note, Waldegrave tackled the question of 'the Rushdie affair', in which the Iranians had put a price on the head of the British-based novelist Salman Rushdie for his book *Satanic Verses*, and 'the Kurdish problem': 'When we met we did agree that neither the Rushdie affair nor the Kurdish problem were issues which the guidelines were drawn up to cover . . .' Neither 'affair' nor 'problem' should be allowed to get in the way of British trade.

The Baghdad Military Exhibition opened on 28 April 1989, which just happened to be Saddam's birthday. It was a great window case for the world's arms industry, with UK Ltd doing its best for the tyrant's treat, short of singing 'Happy Birthday, dear Saddam'.

The tone of the fair was set from the very beginning. Instead of Saddam blowing out the candles on a cake, his guards blew an aircraft out of the sky. An unfortunate Egyptian pilot flew over the presidential palace by mistake and was shot down by the oerlikons of the ever-zealous presidential anti-aircraft battery. According to Kenneth R. Timmerman, the Alphajet the pilot was flying 'crashed into a residential area of Baghdad, killing twenty people. The pilot and his navigator were seriously injured when they ejected.'

To make the party go with a swing, the British government had ensured that as many firms could exhibit at the fair as possible. The programme carried an impressive list of British companies: Astra Holdings PLC, British Aerospace, the Defence Manufacturers Association, Errut, GEC Avionics, Graviner Ltd, Mantech Ltd, Matrix Churchill, Olympus KMI, Racal, Rapid Metal Developments, Rolls-Royce Ltd, Rotabroach, Strumech Engineerind [*sic*], Thorn EMI and United Scintific [*sic*] Holdings. The exhibition guide was decorated with an Iraqi flag eclipsing a hot desert sun, with the numerals '89' to the fore. The top part of the '8' had been decorated with a sniper's sight so that no one missed the exhibition's purpose.

Henderson was at the exhibition, selling his machine tools and doing a little bit of spying on the side. Henderson had met

Balson from MI6 on 24 April 1989 at his office. The MI6 report records:

> Henderson smiled and said that he was expecting a visit. When [section deleted, presumably Balson] explained his specific interest in Iraqi nuclear, chemical-biological, and missile procurement, Henderson said he would do what he could to help. Henderson said that he would be visiting the Baghdad Military Exhibition and that he would be prepared to look out for interests.

At least one British spy was at the Baghdad arms bazaar, but so were a battery of civil servants. Salesmen from the MOD outlet, the Defence Export Services Organization (DESO), were allowed to go to the fair, but with the ministerial proviso that their presence be discreet. On 2 February 1989, civil servant D. F. Weidner, for Lord Trefgarne, minuted: 'Lord Trefgarne was content for DESO representatives to attend this exhibition in Baghdad provided the embassy was kept abreast of our proposals. However, again there should be no DESO stand at the exhibition.' (The 'again' was a reference to Trefgarne's approval, noted earlier in the 2 February 1989 document, to DESO staff going to a similar arms bazaar in Tehran, so long as there was no DESO stand for 'obvious reasons. Attendance by DESO representatives in civilian clothes however was acceptable.') This was consistent with what Alan Clark has subsequently described as 'Whitehall cosmetics'.

If there is one single document that skewers the British government's claims over arms sales to Iraq, it is the four-page list, dated 21 March 1989, of British defence equipment requiring export licences prior to their display at Saddam's birthday bazaar. The list of working equipment, dummies and models was approved by Whitehall, with a few exceptions for security reasons. Here are some of the highlights of the list that went before the civil servants for their approval. Nearly everything was.

'Iraq: Baghdad International Exhibition for Military Production – 28 April to 2 May.'

From BMARC, a defence firm based in Grantham, Lincolnshire, graphic displays of 20-mm, 25-mm, 30-mm, 35-mm cannons, 20-mm and 30-mm naval gun mountings, 20-mm to 60-mm ammunition, fuses and pyrotechnics, sectioned dummies of the above and different types of ammunition, inert dummies of 60-mm mortar bomb, 81-mm mortar bomb and practice shells. From 'Thorm [sic] EMI', graphic displays for the MRF and the Cymbeline defence systems. From Matrix Churchill, computer numerically controlled lathes. From British Aerospace (Dynamics), models of the Rapier Blindfire, the Rapier Laserfire Pallet, the Skyflash Missile, the Merlin Mortar Bomb, the Hawk 60 trainer jet, the Hawk 200 trainer jet, the Tornado ADV, the Harrier II GR5, the Tornado IDS, the 146-STA and brochures of the Sea Archer 1A, the Sea Archer 30 and the AMHS defence system.

From United Scientific Holdings, graphic displays of the Nighthawk, the Laser Rangefinder TL10, the Starfire and others; actual equipment: mine detectors, aiming circle beacon, artillery CPO equipment, muzzle boresight, anti-aircraft sight, turret systems, grenade launcher, laser target marker . . .

From Vinten Ltd, video camera systems; from Mantech Ltd, vehicle engine parts; from Graviner Ltd, vehicle crewbay fire protection systems; from J. and S. Franklin Ltd, optical and night vision equipment; from Pilatus Britten Norman, the Islander AEW aircraft.

The civil servants made a few deletions here and there on security grounds, fearful that British technology might leak through Iraq to the Soviet enemy. Whitehall required that some of the more sensitive technology be returned to Britain at the end of the exhibition. But no one in the British defence business would have suspected for a moment that the government was not broadly encouraging defence sales to Iraq. After all, not only were the government's own DESO salesmen present at the show but also the MOD had allowed civil servant David Hastie, a former executive with British Aerospace, to go to Baghdad, temporarily seconded to his old firm to oversee that Britain did not miss any tricks. Hastie even got to meet Habobi's boss and Waldegrave's conversation partner, Hussein Kamil, in the British bid to sell its arms to Iraq. Hastie was quoted in Timmerman's book, *The Death Lobby*, as telling the journalist at the fair: 'What Saddam really wants are American fighter planes. I guess he figures that buying British is the next best thing, a way of getting his foot in the door.' Timmerman quoted Hastie as saying that Hussein was particularly impressed to learn that British Aerospace had been selected by the US Navy to train pilots for the Hawk. 'That is what the Iraqis want. They want American-style training, American-style tactics, American-standard aircraft. If they can't get them from the United States, then they will get them from us.'

Official encouragement to sell defence equipment to Iraq was a source of comfort to British businessmen who went to Baghdad, like Peter Allen of Matrix Churchill. He told BBC's *Panorama*, broadcast on 3 September 1990: 'We exhibited there [the Baghdad Military Exhibition] for a number of reasons. One was we had active Government support. We were sponsored by the British Overseas Trade Board along with a number of other British companies. You have to remember that Iraq is not a terribly sophisticated country in media terms and therefore you use whatever method you can to promote your products. We have no problem with having sold to Iraq because . . . all of our products had the correct licences and the correct approvals. We were actively encouraged by the government to go there.'

The presence of a British Aerospace team trying to sell the Hawk aircraft to Saddam had a great morale-boosting effect for those in Whitehall pressing for unrestricted trade with Iraq. MOD civil servant Allen Barrett minuted on 6 March 1989: 'If BAe are allowed to take the Hawk, then other companies must be allowed to take their equipment (subject to export licence of course).' Those inside Whitehall who may have argued that trading with Saddam was wrong lacked all conviction.

Tyranny craves respect. Any nasty regime can bully and torture its people into going through the motions, taking care to imprison, execute and even gas-bomb its perceived enemies. But the quality which for ever eludes the tyrant is the respect of the free, those who do not cower under his whip. That is why the pages of the *Baghdad Observer* are full of lengthy reports of visits by otherwise minor Western politicians, which we can now read for our enlightenment on those who kow-towed before Saddam's dictatorship.

It was only a throwaway paragraph in the 30 May 1989 edition of the *Daily Telegraph*, a story of no great importance, headlined 'Iraq agreement': 'Mr David Mellor, Health Minister, signed an agreement with Iraq yesterday on health service co-operation, including exchange visits and medical training – Reuter.'

'Reuter' is the clue. The international news agency would not file on this kind of story had it originated in Britain. But 'Reuter' meant that Mellor must have signed the agreement in Baghdad itself. No other quality national newspaper in Britain carried this paragraph, but, true to form, the *Baghdad Observer* gives it pride of place. On 28 May 1989, the paper's lead story on page 2 was: 'British health secretary starts visit to Iraq', illustrated with a picture of Mellor, his mouth open, in mid-speech. The *Baghdad Observer* reported:

> Mr Mellor told the *Baghdad Observer*, during his tour of the Medical City complex in Baghdad, that the objective of his visit is to strengthen ties between Iraq and Britain in the field of health services.
>
> 'There is a long-time tradition of co-operation between Iraq and Britain. A large number of Iraqi doctors get their training in Britain,' Mr Mellor said . . .

The report added that this was Mellor's third visit to Iraq. He had been before in 1982 and 1988. It went on to quote the health minister: '"What can be of great importance to our co-operation is that both countries have identical health system [*sic*], namely the national health service. This common philosophy enables both sides to organize their means of co-operating towards one aim."'

'Common philosophy'? 'Both countries have . . . the national health service'? What could Mellor have been talking about? Criticized though the British national health service may be, its practices have yet to be cited in Amnesty International reports on cruel and unusual torture. Mellor and his advisers at the Department of Health might have cared to read the Amnesty document 'Torture in Iraq', April 1985, before giving the Iraqi health service such a glowing tribute in the *Baghdad Observer*. Case number five in that document cites the following evidence:

An Iraqi doctor of medicine testified to Amnesty International in 1984 that he witnessed and was forced to participate in the taking of blood from prisoners which resulted in their death. According to his testimony, he was aware of approximately 1000 such operations having taken place during 1982 and 1983. The operations are reportedly directly controlled by Security Headquarters (Ri'asat al-Mukhabarat) in Baghdad, and carried out with the co-operation of a prison director and personnel of the Blood Bank Institute in Baghdad. The following are extracts from his testimony:

'At Abu Ghraib prison in Baghdad . . . where I was told there are . . . donors who want to donate blood . . . the prison doctor took me to the prison hospital. I found there two persons in a state of shock, immobile and who exhibited air hunger with rapid thready pulse and cold clammy skin. The prison doctor told me these two were criminals and that he bled them under the influence of hypnotic drugs in order to benefit from their blood before they are executed. This doctor also told me that he has directives from Security Headquarters to use this method with important political persons so as to give the reason for the subsequent death as "heart failure". The directive also applies to criminals sentence to death.'

On another occasion at the same prison:

'The prison doctor . . . told me that he will bleed three persons and asked me to help him. When I refused, he told me the Security Headquarters demanded that this operation must be done under my supervision and that if I refused they will jail me.'

Amnesty asked a British haematologist to study the Iraqi doctor's testimony. The haematologist concluded that the victims' symptoms were what one would have expected if they had been drained of a substantial amount of blood. The British doctor added: 'If this statement is true then it is not in accord with the directives of the World Health Organization or any other reputable international or national body involved with blood donation and transfusion.'

The *Baghdad Observer* reported that Mellor and his health officials visited Baghdad's 'Medical City'. If they were intending to carry out a thorough investigation of Iraq's medical services, they might have asked to see the Medical City Mortuary. Case number three of the 1985 Amnesty 'Torture in Iraq' report cites the testimony of a mother of a fourth-year medical student from Basra, who was asked by 'security men' to pick up the 'carcass' of her son at the Medical City Mortuary. She told Amnesty International:

When I entered and saw what was inside, I could not believe that there are people who could do such things to other human beings . . . My son was not in the refrigerator but was thrown on the floor of one of the rooms . . . I looked around and saw nine bodies stretched out on the floor with him . . . but my son was in a chair form . . . that is a sitting form, not sleeping or stretched. He had blood all over him and his body was very eaten away and bleeding. I looked at the others stretched out on the floor alongside him . . . all burnt . . . I don't know with what . . . another's body carried the marks of a hot domestic iron all over his head to his feet . . . another one was burnt in such a way, even his hair, like someone who had been incinerated . . . and every one was burnt in a different way . . .'

The staff of Britain's NHS may be badly paid and demoralized, but when compared with its Iraqi sister our service does come out rather better, in fact, magnificently so. Mellor and his advisers might have cared to read the 22 September 1988 edition of the *New Scientist*, which covered the Iraqi health service's treatment of Kurdish victims of poison gas, citing Kurdish sources for their report:

> After the [mustard gas bomb] attacks in 1987, 368 Kurdish civilians sought medical help in the main hospitals of the major cities – Sulaimaniya, Kirkuk and Irbil. The authorities instructed the hospitals to refuse treatment, unless the victim first signed a statement to say that it was Iran that had attacked them with gas. Later, all 368 were arrested and sent to prison in Irbil where they were executed.

Contrary to Mellor's view that there was a 'common philosophy' in Britain and Iraq, the evidence suggests that the Iraqi health service was, like everything else, bent to serve the central, organizing philosophy of the tyrant's sadism.

It is, of course, possible that Mellor was misquoted by the Iraqi newspaper. But Mellor has been justly praised for his fluency and his media technique, characterized, perhaps unfairly, by one wit recorded in Roth's *Parliamentary Profiles* as: 'relentless sincerity larded with an excessive and oleaginous use of the interviewer's Christian name'. So why did he not make ample use of the British media he normally uses so well to condemn the poor journalistic standards of the *Baghdad Observer*?

Moreover, there seems no doubt that Mellor did sign the health agreement with Iraq, as reported by Reuter, and, in turn, by the *Daily Telegraph* on 30 May 1989. The act of signing such an agreement automatically conferred a degree of respect and respectability on Iraq. As far as the then British minister of health and his advisers were concerned Iraq was not an international pariah state.

Curiously, he did not appear willing to discuss any of his three separate trips to Iraq. It was difficult to get in touch with him. A number of telephone calls were made in early December. On 14 December 1992, another message was left at the House of

Commons for him; and again the next day. On 17 December, someone at his office declined an interview on his behalf: 'He's too busy to talk. He's overloaded with the National Lottery. He's not even ringing the BBC back, so it's unlikely he'll ring back someone who's writing a book.'

But there can be no doubt that Mellor had the measure of Saddam's tyranny. He told two MPs from the Campaign Against the Repression of Democratic Rights in Iraq (CARDRI) on 12 April 1988, when he was still a minister at the Foreign Office, that he was aware of the nature of the Iraqi regime since both of his hosts during the 1982 visit to Iraq (one of whom was the mayor of Baghdad) had been shot dead in power struggles prior to his 1988 visit.

So why did he go back in 1989? Putting on one side his enthusiasm for the Iraqi health service, it seems likely that he wanted to play another round of the 'constant hostage syndrome' game. Waldegrave had been unlucky, but perhaps Mellor fancied his ability to spring Ian Richter from Abu Ghraib prison. This might explain why, according to the *Baghdad Observer*, 30 May 1989, Mellor not only met the acting Iraqi minister of health, Abdul Salam Mohammed Sa'eed, but also Saddam's foreign minister, Tareq Aziz. Whatever Mellor's motive, he, too, returned empty-handed, while the tyranny pocketed the new-found international respect for its health service. The Iraqis, once again, had the better of a visit from a British minister.

There is a strange coda to this visit. In House of Commons debates and in replies to protesting letters, government ministers made much of Mellor's tough stance with the Iraqis after his February 1988 visit. For example, on 21 September 1988, Waldegrave wrote to Lord Avebury making clear the government's 'firm stance' on reports of Iraqi abuses of human rights. He added: 'When David Mellor visited Iraq in February [1988], he took the opportunity to raise the issue of human rights and left the Iraqi regime in no doubt about our views.' But on the available evidence it seems that no minister or civil servant made reference to the 1989 Mellor trip, either in Parliament or outside it. A computer search of the British quality daily newspaper press in May and June 1989 showed no coverage of the Anglo-Iraq health agreement. The only mention, missed by the computer, was in the *Daily Telegraph* paragraph. That came from Reuters, which picked up the health agreement story not from Whitehall but from Iraq. It seems, on the face of it, as if the normally publicity-hungry minister and his civil servants did not choose to inform British newspapers of his third trip to Iraq. However, this is supposition.

It seems, on the face of it, difficult to reconcile his condemnation of the Iraqi use of poison gas, after Halabja, when on 30 March 1988 he told the House of Commons: 'It now seems clear that chemical weapons were used by Iraq against its own Kurdish population and the Iranian invaders. That use was contrary to international obligations entered into by Iraq . . .' with his making a not-very-well-publicized international agreement with the Iraqis the following year.

For all students of Anglo-Iraq relations it is a regret that Mellor, even though he is no longer a minister, could not find time to discuss Britain and Iraq's common health philosophy because he was so burdened with the vexatious question of the 'National Lottery'. This too is supposition.

CHAPTER
SEVEN

One explanation for John Major's role in the Iraqgate scandal appeared in print as follows:

> When Mr Waldegrave brought in the tea and Viennese whirls at 11 o'clock, I put on my special stern voice and asked him why he hadn't told me about the Superglue affair on 13th July 1989 as that bearded Labour man Mr Cook keeps saying.
>
> 'We didn't tell you because in those days you were just some silly little twit who no one thought was going to be prime minister,' he said. Everyone laughed.
>
> At first I was in no small measure prepared to be quite annoyed at this, but then Mr Hurd pointed out that this was a very convenient admission by Mr Waldegrave as it let me off the hook completely. When Mr Waldegrave left the room, Mr Hurd dialled the police and told them to investigate Mr Waldegrave at once since he was as much to blame for this whole sorry mess as Mr Clark.

Thus 'The Secret Diary of John Major, aged 47¾' in *Private Eye*, 4 December 1992.

Such a squib might appear unfair to a politician who prides himself upon his mastery of detail. But when one sifts and weighs the evidence of what Major knew and/or must have known as a rising star in the Thatcher administration about Britain's secret arming of Iraq, the *Private Eye* lampoon looks rather generous.

Major replaced Sir Geoffrey Howe as foreign secretary on 25 July 1989, in a power play by Mrs Thatcher which ultimately exploded in her face. Newspaper and political comment has concentrated on Major's role in Iraqgate from this date onwards, forgetful that as chief secretary to the Treasury he helped to create the financial foundations for the arming of Iraq. (Page 6 of the current Cabinet Office Machinery of Government Guidelines states that the chief secretary is the Treasury minister responsible for export credits.) As chief secretary he effectively signed the cheques for the British government's medium term export credits to Iraq, making over £175 million of taxpayers' money in 1987 (for 1988) and £340 million in 1988 (for 1989), 'insuring' those firms who traded with Iraq, plus millions of pounds' worth of short term credits. A good fifth of those trade credits were set aside for defence sales. On 16 November 1987, J. M. Foster of the Export Credits Guarantee Department (ECGD) minuted to the MOD a document headed: 'Credit for Defence Sales to Iraq'. He wrote: 'A notional 20 per cent allocation [of the total trade credits] has been set aside for military business.' It was Major's job to look over the public purse and see that no money was wasted on risky or fruitless gambles – as the export credits to Iraq turned out to be.

In 1987 and 1988 chief secretary Major oversaw a dramatic expansion in the trade credits for Iraqi business, including defence sales. He was not a peripheral player in this business, but its (politically answerable) insurer.

Throughout the first half of 1989, during the time Major was chief secretary and after, when he was replaced by Norman Lamont, now chancellor of the exchequer, the alarm bells started to ring that the risks might outweigh the premium. Whereas many in the Iraqgate scandal chose to hide behind Sir Geoffrey Howe's 'but not conclusive' formula when confronted with evidence that upset the smooth progress of defence equipment to Iraq, the civil servants in the ECGD had a duty to make a few simple checks before risking millions of pounds' worth of tax-payers' money. The civil servants operating the Howe guidelines issued export licences for defence equipment to Iraq so long as it did not 'significantly enhance' and so on and so forth; the ECGD men were insuring against risks. To do their job properly, they had to discover the precise nature of those risks.

They did not like what they found. They discovered suspicions that the Matrix Churchill machine tools could be going to munitions factories, that the exports to Iraq were via a Chilean arms/chemical manufacturer and, most disagreeable of all, that the goods 'were destined to Iraq, to be incorporated into a chemical weapons factory'.

The alarm bells clamoured away, but no one in the corridors of power appeared to be listening.

None of the ECGD paperwork released through the Matrix Churchill case has the name or office of Major or Lamont or any other minister on their distribution lists, only other civil servants. Although we know that the Whitehall weeders from the Cabinet Office deleted, blacked out and removed politically sensitive correspondence from the sequence of documents – for example, Mrs Thatcher's letter on trade with Iraq of 2 September 1988 – there is no evidence that any minister knew of the concerns of the government's own underwriters. Yet the minutes and correspondence from the underwriters show that some in government were only too well aware of the risks of trading with Iraq.

The first alarm bell rang in early August 1988, during the time of Saddam's summer gas offensive against the Kurds, when Matrix Churchill applied for ECGD cover for a £6.5 million contract for forty-eight machine tools for Industrias Cardoen, of Los Conquistadores, Santiago, Chile. There was no mention of Iraq on the application form, numbered CXT 53921X/0276 and date stamped 3 August 1988. Being conscientious custodians of the public purse, the ECGD civil servants in the Credit Information Branch immediately checked out the buyer. The ECGD civil servants asked a Chilean credit agency to report on Cardoen's activities. The Chilean credit agency described Cardoen as 'manufacturer and distributor of explosives, chemical substances and military vehicles and elements'. The ECGD men organized cover for £6.5 million which was approved on 20 October 1988.

But Cardoen was no ordinary manufacturer of explosives and chemical substances. Labour MP Ken Livingstone told the House of Commons on 27 November 1992 of an allegation in a book, *The Profits of War* (of which more later) that: 'Mark Thatcher [the son of the then serving prime minister] was an associate of Dr Carlos Cardoen . . . [whose] main job in life was the procurement of arms for Iraq in the West.' There is no evidence that the civil servants within ECGD knew anything of the Mark Thatcher allegations at the time or since or that the allegations are true.

The second alarm bell went off on 11 November 1988, when the *Financial Times* printed a story about Cardoen. The ECGD read the piece with distinct unease and referred back to it in subsequent correspondence. Barbara Durr reported:

> The weapons conglomerate Industrias Cardoen, chief supplier to the Iraqi airforce during the war, has been forced to convert to diversified non-military products and engineering services. But its business with Iraq is hardly over . . . Its most controversial contribution to Iraq in this regard is construction of a weapons factory, where Western intelligence sources say the Iraqis are building chemical weapons . . .
>
> Although Mr Raul Montesino, spokesman for the company, denies that Cardoen produces or has produced chemical weapons, among the companies reported to be in its Chilean group is Exploqulm, a chemical explosives factory . . . The company's [admitted] military products have included cluster bombs, hand grenades, various types of aerial bombs including high fragmentation and delayed action bombs, armoured vehicles, helicopters, anti-personnel and anti-tank mines, torpedoes and demolition charges . . .

The *FT* article reports, flatly, Cardoen's 'construction of a weapons factory, where Western intelligence sources say the Iraqis are building chemical weapons'. There is no mention of an intelligence report on these lines in the Matrix Churchill intelligence documents. During the Matrix Churchill trial, the following exchange took place between Geoffrey Robertson and the MI5 man, Ford, discussing Gutteridge's intelligence reports.

Robertson: In addition the Iraqis are also purchasing other equipment including tooling and chemicals. Is it fair to say that Mr Gutteridge was not able to give you any assistance about chemicals?

Ford: No, that is not true. He did give me some interesting leads on chemicals.

Consider the following points: the poison gas made at the Muthanna gasworks needed to go into munitions, aircraft bombs and artillery shells. Someone had to make those bombs and shells. They had to be well made. Gutteridge may well have picked up some interesting information on this subject, but the trial was stopped before he could enter the witness box.

The *Financial Times* article is not proof positive of a Western intelligence report that says that Cardoen was building a factory in which the Iraqis were making munitions for chemical weapons, but it is a reliable enough source to spark unease. The article was not specific about which factory in Iraq was making chemical weapons. Cardoen's operations in the country were spread across a good number of facilities. The newspaper report certainly worried the civil servants answerable to chief secretary Major.

The third alarm bell rang on 29 November 1988. Stephen Lillie of the Foreign Office's Middle East Department informed his boss Tim Simmons that the ECGD people had discovered something else unsettling. Lillie minuted that a 'Mr McKibbin of ECGD in Cardiff' told him that he, McKibbin, had been informed that 'Matrix Churchill have exported lathe equipment to Chile worth £6.5 million which they have then sent on to Iraq'. Lillie noted that the DTI 'have no record of any licensable exports by Matrix Churchill to Chile since 1985'. The civil servant surmised:

This would suggest that:
(i) the reports are unfounded; or

(ii)   the equipment was not licensable anyway; or

(iii) Matrix have exported illegally.

That much was a false alarm. The phrase 'have exported lathe eqiupment' was unfounded because Matrix Churchill had not yet exported the machine tools. However, the ECGD's information that the machine tools were being bought by Cardoen for shipment direct to Iraq – the first mention in the Matrix Churchill paper chase – was accurate. Matrix Churchill had not disclosed in their August 1988 application for ECGD cover that the goods bought by Cardoen were going to Iraq. There is no evidence that Matrix Churchill then knew that Iraq was the ultimate destination. At this time, no one at the DTI seemed very bothered by this omission. Later, after the invasion, the Cardoen contract made up part of the case against the Matrix Churchill Three, who were, of course, found not guilty by the jury.

Lillie's minute – correct about the goods going to Iraq, wrong about their having already gone – was copied to COMED, the Commerce and Exports Department in the FCO and PUSD, which stands for Permanent Under-Secretaries Department – Whitehall hey-nonny-no for MI6. I give these details because it shows just how many people in Whitehall were conscious of the problems relating to Matrix Churchill's trade with Iraq via Cardoen. No doubt at some stage Lillie would have minuted a correction to his original minute, çopied to the spooks.

The fourth alarm bell went off on 20 January 1989, when a civil servant from the ECGD minuted to K. Illingworth of the Insurance Services Underwriters (ISU) in Cardiff, under the title: 'Matrix Churchill Ltd, Industrias Cardoen Ltda, Chile'. The civil servant – in the context, perhaps someone from the ECGD's Birmingham Regional Office – wrote after a meeting with insurance broker Robert Lemin of the Birmingham branch office of Sedgwick's, that the goods

will be going to Iraq . . . Brokers suspect that the goods will be used to manufacture munitions, and these munitions and possibly oil will be used to pay for the goods supplied . . . if in view of the full facts now available you are willing to take on this [word too faint to read, perhaps deleted] business, they would prefer us to issue a fresh approval to cover both contracts ... There is an element of foreign goods in both contracts ... The goods are CNC lathes from Japan or Switzerland, which are not available in this country ... There is a potential problem here, as policyholders used to be part of the TI group but they have been recently bought out by a group called the TMG group who have Iraqi backing, which is probably why this business has come their way ...

The question as to *why* the broker 'suspected' that goods made by an Iraqi-owned machine tools firm to be sent to Iraq (via a manufacturer of explosives and chemical substances in Chile said by Western intelligence sources to be constructing a munitions factory for Iraqi chemical weapons) 'will be used to manufacture munitions' *did* trouble the civil servants answerable to chief secretary Major.

The fifth alarm bell was remarkably loud. It was a minute, its contents overlooked by many who followed the great Matrix Churchill paper chase because it is hand-written. (Students of Anglo-Iraq trade with suspicious minds might wonder whether there was a typewritten version of this and other subsequent minutes from the ECGD which was somehow redacted in favour of the infinitely more difficult to read version scribbled by hand.) The date is indistinct, but the minute refers to an application which 'arrived on my desk around 3.00 p.m.' on 20 January 1989 and the context places it firmly in that month. The minute is from S. (or G.) Matthews, an ECGD civil servant in the ISU:

(i) Matrix Churchill initially came in for cover on this arms/ chemical manufacturer [Cardoen] in August 1988. We approved cover for CV of £6.5 million approx.

(ii) We later learnt that the buyer is a chief supplier of the Iraqi air force and had been built up on the back of this business. It seems they are involved 'in chemical weapons manufacture' ...

The ECGD men wanted out. Matthews's colleague, Illingworth, summed up the feelings within the ECGD in a sloping hand on 24 January 1988:

> The view is taken that some way should be found to withdraw from the business. This may be done:
> (a) on straight creditworthiness grounds;
> (b) because of the Iraqi risk;
> (c) by imposing a hefty surcharge;
> (d) [unreadable].

His colleague J. McKibbin minuted by hand the following day:

> Because this case is complicated due to the many factors involved, principally the Iraqi risk and the nature/use of the goods, I think we should meet to discuss what to do.

One of the ECGD civil servants minuted, on 31 January 1989, that he had spoken with Tim Simmons at the Foreign Office, 'who advises that Matrix Churchill goods are the subject of an investigation by the FCO [Foreign and Commonwealth Office] and the DTI and the case is at present with ministers for decision . . .'

And then? The alarms fell silent; or, rather, the paperwork from the ECGD men answerable to chief secretary Major stops in late January 1989 with their unease about insuring the Cardoen contract very apparent.

However, there is a document, unweeded, which sums up what happened next. It is the hidden 'crown jewels' of the Matrix Churchill treasure. The 'crown jewels' is a background briefing paper in handwriting so dreadful that it is no wonder it was overlooked. It is dated 24 August 1989: that is, after the time Norman Lamont took over as the Treasury minister responsible for export credits. However, the 24 August 'crown jewels' relates the story of what decisions were taken on the prickly question of insuring the Cardoen contract when Major was still at the Treasury.

The document is from Matthews to Illingworth of the ISU.

Customer: Matrix Churchill; contract value £6.5 m(illion); goods: machine tools . . . Matrix Churchill initially came in for CXT cover August 88 when £6.5 m(illion) was approved (C167) with credit over five years from date of each shift. This approval was given based [it looks like 'based'] on financial figures of buyer, its sector (military vehicles) – in a belief that goods were for buyer's own use.

We then received a further application for £7.4 m(illion) . . . and more details on both contracts. Goods were destined for Iraq, to be incorporated into a chemical weapons factory . . . C167 was finally cancelled and replaced by a CST credit limit for £4 m(illion) on terms of 20 days by pre-accepted bills of exchange.

Just to ensure there was no mistaking the point, Matthews repeated it at the end of his handwritten note, arguing for 'some proof of end-buyer's (in previous case Iraqi chemical weapons factory) ability to pay'.

Another civil servant – from the context, probably Illing-worth – adds immediately below: 'Please see background sub-mission done by Mr Matthews above . . . At the end of the day we underwrote £4 m(illion) on 15.3.1989 on [word indistinct] 180 day terms.'

The civil servants delayed a decision on the second Matrix Churchill application for insurance. But it is clear from the ECGD documents of 24 August 1989 that the British government had provided insurance on the first Matrix Churchill application, underwriting £4 million on 15 March 1989, on goods that a civil servant stated flatly were bound for an Iraqi 'chemical weapons factory'.

This statement is not a leak in a newspaper or a remark made by a conspiracy-minded trouble-maker, but the careful assessment of a conscientious career civil servant on top of his brief. Nor was the statement made in isolation. On 1 November 1990, the ECGD's regional director in Birmingham, Paul St. J. Miller, reviewed the known facts in a letter headed 'Matrix Churchill: Industrias Cardoen Ltda – Chile'. Miller described how initially Matrix Churchill applied for credit cover in August 1988 for £6.5 million over five years. He continued: '2. A further application for £7.4 million [ECGD reference] (C168) was then received providing more details on both contracts. Goods were apparently destined for Iraq to be incorporated into a chemical weapons factory.'

In January 1989 the ECGD civil servants proposed four separate ways of dropping the Cardoen business. Three months later they approved insurance cover. Did the civil servants consult ministers before they made the 15 March 1989 decision? There is no evidence that ministers knew of their concerns.

The Chilean connection caused no end of worry to a lot of people in Whitehall, even among the champions of trade with Iraq, the civil servants of the DTI. For example, a note addressed to Steadman, dated 31 March 1989, shows: 'TIR overland to Iraq and an agent in Chile has all the hallmarks of a suspect transaction.'

Someone with some sympathy for that view is the Labour MP, Ken Livingstone. After the collapse of the Matrix Churchill case, Livingstone told the House of Commons on 27 November 1989, about *Profits of War*, a 'book that had been published in America by a former Israeli military intelligence officer, Ari Ben-Menashe. The book could not be published in Britain because of our restrictive libel laws. It contained damaging revelations about Mark Thatcher and arms sales to Iraq . . .' (One is free, however, to publish speeches to the House of Commons without fear or favour.)

Livingstone continued:

I accept that we have to be careful when dealing with the revelations of rogue intelligence officers who have turned against their former employer . . . The author makes various charges. The book stated that Mark Thatcher owned a Texas-based company that was used to move equipment directly from

Britain to Iraq ... The book also alleges that Mark Thatcher was an associate of Dr Carlos Cardoen ... According to Ari Ben-Menashe, Dr Cardoen's main job in life was the procurement of arms for Iraq in the West. When Ari Ben-Menashe – who was then still working for Israeli intelligence and trying to discourage Gerald Bull from going ahead with the supergun – arrived at Dr Cardoen's office, he found Mark Thatcher there. What was Mark Thatcher doing with Iraq's main procurer of weapons in the West? The book alleges that Dr Cardoen was introduced to Mr Bull by Mark Thatcher, who was the link person. If these allegations are true, they are breathtaking.

Indeed. (It must be noted, however, that none have been substantiated.)

According to Simon Henderson's *Instant Empire*, in Cardoen's Santiago office a picture of Saddam was hung on the wall and remained there until after the invasion of Kuwait.

The Matrix Churchill British spies Paul Henderson (no relation to Simon) and Mark Gutteridge left the British intelligence officers they reported to in no doubt that Cardoen was playing a big part in the arming of Iraq. In the trial the following exchange took place between Robertson and the MI5 man, Ford:

ROBERTSON (*reading from secret documents*): And that Mr Gutteridge is reporting that someone in December 1988 ... told him that the Chilean project covered not only a range of fuses but also [made] mention of 210-mm shells and missiles.
FORD: Yes.

Robertson, drawing on information about Gutteridge who was assisting the defence, asked Ford about a meeting which took place in Baghdad in November 1988.

ROBERTSON: You recall a meeting where you talked about ... the International Exhibition in Baghdad in November 1988 ... One of the things he told you was he had actually met Carlos Cardoen himself on the steps of the al-Rashid Hotel where he was staying. And had been introduced to him by Mr Henderson, who was with Mr Gutteridge.

Former chief secretary Major has always made political capital out of his command of detail. During the 1992 general election, he would buttonhole his interviewers, and press them to ask him on the detail. However, ministers are busy people, pressed for time. There is no evidence that the serving chief secretary knew that in March 1989 the ECGD insured goods believing them to be destined for an Iraqi 'chemical weapons factory'.

However, if one forgets the details and looks at the big picture in the first part of 1989, what was obvious to many in the world's financial centres was that Iraq was having trouble paying its bills. Saddam owed Kuwait and Saudi Arabia $35 billion, the rest of the world a similiar figure, making a round total debt of $70 billion. The oil price was weak and, according to Kenneth Timmerman, 'he had mortgaged Iraq's future for two generations by selling long-term oil contracts in order to buy weapons.' In the idiom of the ECGD for which chief secretary Major was responsible to the taxpayer, Saddam was not a good risk.

Once he was made foreign secretary, however, Major's role in Britain's arming of Iraq became even more important. Britain was arming Saddam, blind to the moral and strategic consequences of the trade. Fundamental changes in our policy towards Iraq were required urgently. Nothing happened. It was steady as she goes, with parliamentary trippers and a Cabinet minister all jumping aboard the Baghdad gravy train. The government's failure to see the mounting dangers to our genuine national security – a failure in which the new foreign secretary played a central part – was to have, for some, murderous consequences.

But Major's part was very much non-speaking, non-acting. As foreign secretary he received the cream of MI6 intelligence analysis, which in the summer of 1989 was inking in some pretty black storm clouds. For example, that August intelligence documents revealed that a British firm, later identified as Matrix Churchill, was helping Saddam upgrade Scud missiles to bring targets in Israel and Saudi Arabia within their range. The documents refer to Project 1728 – the Iraqi plan to extend the Scuds' range. As far as one can tell, the new foreign secretary left such concerns to his junior minister William Waldegrave.

The intelligence reports and analyses released through the Matrix Churchill case are not only heavily blacked out but sketchy and erratic. By deduction, however, it is possible to glean something of the mood of the intelligence community in Whitehall about Britain's arming of Iraq in 1989: increasingly gloomy. Take a report from the Defence Intelligence Staff (DIS) headlined 'British Assistance to the Emerging Iraqi Arms Industry'. It was sent to Alan Clark who had moved from trade to defence procurement in July 1989, following a neat job swap with Lord Trefgarne. The foreign secretary might not have read every word of the DIS report – might not even have seen it – but he would have heard the tune. The DIS warned:

> The amount of assistance that 'UK Ltd', in particular our machinery manufacturers, are giving to Iraq towards the set-up of a major arms R&D and production industry [represented] a very significant enhancement to the ability of Iraq to manufacture its own arms thus to resume the war with Iran . . . All it needs is for an investigative journalist to pull together the threads. The minister should be made aware of this unfolding situation, since it could reach the press.

Originally, this analysis was unclassified, but following the invasion of Kuwait and the heightened media interest in how Iraq came to be so powerfully armed, the report's classification was changed on 3 December 1990, to 'restricted'. By that stage the Iraqi horse had bolted; the only reason for restricting the report was to keep the public from knowing the stable door had been wide open all along.

Major himself said in the House of Commons debate following the collapse of the Matrix Churchill trial that the argument over continued shipment of the firm's machine tools to Iraq was conducted by his junior minister William Waldegrave. As the summer of 1989 moved into the autumn, the Foreign Office in the guise of Waldegrave took a stronger line with the DTI. In the phrase made familiar by Arthur Scargill, the Foreign Office decided to get off its knees and fight.

The first victory came easily. Mrs Thatcher shot down the Hawk project. A source who was acquainted with what happened at the Cabinet committee concerned, which met in the summer of 1989, recalled: 'It was very funny. Alan Clark was cock-a-hoop because the Archbishop of Canterbury had been on the radio that very morning, arguing against British selling Hawk aircraft to Iraq because of Saddam's abysmal human rights record. Clark was going round Whitehall saying: "If that c*** Runcie is against the sale, then we've won. Maggie is bound to say yes." In the event, the prime minister turned to the item on the agenda, shook her head and said something like: "I don't think that's a very good idea. Next." Clark was gob-smacked. He couldn't swing it, even if it meant Maggie burying her instincts and siding with the Church of England.' The source says the meeting took place around the time but probably before Major became foreign secretary, but does not recall Major, if present, making a significant enhancement to the debate: 'There wasn't any.' Another source commented on the decision: 'There are limits to what British public opinion can stomach. If we had sold Saddam those planes, we could not have been sure that he would not have used them to gas-bomb the Kurds again. That would have been too embarrassing for words.'

The next development was also embarrassing to those who believed there was nothing to lose by trading with Iraq. The crock of gold at the bottom of the Iraqi arms procurement rainbow turned out to be full of unpleasantness. Throughout the eighties, Iraq's arms buyers had routed their business through the tiny Atlanta branch of an Italian bank, the Banca Nazionale del Lavoro (BNL). The bank's manager, Christopher Drogoul, New Jersey-born of Franco-German-Lebanese origin, was arrested after an FBI raid on 4 August 1989. He admitted forwarding $4 billion dollars' worth of loans to Iraq, money the bank didn't have.

Matthews at the ECGD was soon on the case. He minuted on 13 September 1989: 'Possible criminal indictment will be brought against Christopher Drogoul who Matrix Churchill admit visited them to discuss financial arrangements for credit to sell to the Iraqis . . .' The civil servant reminded his colleagues of who actually owned Matrix Churchill: 'TMG Engineering, a UK-registered company backed by Iraqi money. The ultimate holding company are Al-Arabi Trading Company. There are Iraqi directors on the board of Matrix. The banks involved in the credit for this business between Iraq and Matrix are Lloyds, Dresdner Bank and [underlined twice] BNL.'

There is no evidence that the new chief secretary at the Treasury responsible for export credits, Norman Lamont, was aware of the civil servants' worries about a $4 billion fraud at the bank that liked to say yes to Saddam.

The next Foreign Office victory was over Learfan, a Belfast high-tech carbon fibre factory which had been bought by a consortium of TDG – Habobi's Iraqi front company – and the Brussels-based Space Research Corporation, the financial vehicle for the Dr Strangelove think-alike Dr Gerald Bull and his supergun. Any sharp businessman knows that setting up in Belfast means that a grateful British government will throw money at you. But it was not to be. Under pressure from the Foreign Office because of concerns about the Iraqi connection, the Northern Ireland Industrial Development Board refused a £2 million grant to Learfan's new owners. It is understood that the Foreign Office pressure came, ultimately, from the Americans, who made it clear that British public funding of the TDG-SRC-Learfan project was not acceptable to them.

It was against this background that Waldegrave – on the record as a voice of British revulsion against 'Iraqi barbarities' – went into battle, sort of. On 24 August 1989, Stephen Lillie of the Foreign Office minuted Waldegrave in a letter that Matrix Churchill exports were 'in contravention' of our policy on defence sales to Iraq. Intriguingly, there is a very thick deletion on the distribution list opposite Waldegrave's name. An additional worry was that the lathes could be used to produce components for a nuclear explosive device. If the Foreign Office won the battle and the licences were refused, he argued, 'the minister could inform them [the company] that we have conclusive evidence that previous shipments of equipment have gone to Iraqi munitions factories. He might add, without elaborating, that we have wider concerns . . .'

Waldegrave wrote to Trefgarne and Clark on 6 September 1989, calling for four more export licence applications from Matrix Churchill to be refused because they breached the Howe guidelines. He wrote:

> You will already be aware of our concerns about Matrix Churchill, which was taken over as part of a procurement network for the Iraqi nuclear, CBW and missile programmes. We know, originally from secret sources, that contrary to the assurances of the manufacturer, its high technology machine tools have been shipped to the major Iraqi munitions establishments.

Waldegrave's reference to CBW – Chemical and Biological Warfare – is evidence that it was not just a civil servant in the ECGD who was concerned about the possibility of British technology ending up in Iraqi chemical weapons factories. Former Iraqi desk man at the Foreign Office, Mark Higson, confirms that everyone there was very worried about Iraq's chemical warfare programme. Saddam had used it, after all.

The fight for a more prudent attitude towards Iraq was on, and it would only be settled when Clark, Trefgarne and Waldegrave met later in the year.

Things were not looking very rosy for enthusiasts of Anglo-Iraq trade that autumn. Alan George writing in the *Observer* and a cast of thousands on the *Financial Times* were delving into the BNL collapse and the Iraqi procurement network with an energy which could only have caused embarrassment in high places.

It was an appropriate time in the minds of some for a goodwill visit to Baghdad – and what better way than a parliamentary trip to Iraq?

'Choo-choo! Choo-choo!'

The *Baghdad Observer* reported on 21 September 1989: 'Aziz meets with British delegation'. The report is on the front page, just to the right of a photograph of a smiling 'President Saddam Hussein' who 'toured an exhibition of gifts presented to him by some Iraqis and Arabs'. The British delegation story reads:

> Deputy prime minister and Foreign Minister Mr Tareq Aziz on Wednesday [20 September 1989] met with a visiting British parliamentary delegation headed by Tony Marloe [*sic*: the correct spelling is Marlow]. During the meeting, Iraqi-British relations and the situation between Iraq and Iran were discussed. Both sides also discussed developments of the Palestinian question and the Lebanese issue.

On the same front page under the headline: 'Iraq, Britain discuss co-operation' the *Baghdad Observer* reported:

> Minister of Industry [and Military Industrialization] Mr [Brigadier] Hussein Kamil Hassan on Wednesday met with the parliamentary delegation of the British Conservative Party headed by Mr T. Marloe [*sic*]. The Minister reviewed the country's industrial development plans and stressed Iraq's desire to enhance co-operation with Britain.

The reports were, in other words, the usual dross.

On the trip which took place between 18 September and 22 September 1989 (no doubt also cleared by the Foreign Office) were, according to Dr Omar al-Hassan of the Gulf Centre for Strategic Studies, Marlow, a consultant to the Gulf Centre, and five other Tory MPs: Nicholas Bennett, the member for Pembroke who lost his seat in the 1992 election, Hugh Dykes, the member for Harrow East, Anthony Nelson, the member for Chichester and now economic secretary at the Treasury, Tim Smith, the member for Beaconsfield and now deputy chairman of the Conservative Party and Timothy Wood, the member for Stevenage. In the Parliamentary *Register of Members' Interests*,

Smith is cited as visiting 'Iraq as guest of the Iraqi government'. Some of the other MPs filed the visit as a guest of the Gulf Centre. All of the MPs had recorded the trip by the time of publication of the 1992 Register, apart from Dykes. He does not mention this trip in the '90, '91 or '92 Register. We were unable to elicit any comment from Dykes despite numerous attempts.

Dr al-Hassan recalled: 'We met Tareq Aziz, Brigadier Hussein Kamil . . . Saddam was busy that time', so the MPs did not get to meet him. No doubt this trip too had been approved by the British Foreign Office. A colourful Baathist functionary whom they did meet was Latif Nassayif Jassim, who reappears in the story as a less than charitable figure later on.

The MPs would naturally have raised with their hosts the plight of the British prisoner/hostage Ian Richter, who was still languishing in jail, which would have been most appreciated by his family. Did Dr al-Hassan have any particular recollection of the MPs as a group raising the Iraqis' serial abuses of human rights with their hosts at every opportunity? Dr Hassan paused before replying. In the silence, my mind went over the gas-bombing of the Kurds, the forced draining of blood from helpless prisoners by the Iraqi national health service, the execution of children . . . Then he replied: 'Not really.' Though that, of course, is not to say that the MPs did not challenge the Iraqi record on human rights abuses when opportunities arose.

The evidence that year on Iraq's human rights abuses was not slim. In February 1989 Amnesty International produced a thirty-three page closely typed report, entitled *Iraq – Children: Innocent Victims of Political Repression*. The following month Amnesty brought out a special pamphlet: *Children brutally treated in Iraq*. Its front cover shows a photograph of a ten-year-old boy, his eyes filled with tears, one of the victims 'of chemical weapon attacks by Iraqi forces'.

One can get a flavour of the pamphlet from the headlines: 'Children are victims of mass killing', 'How Trifa was poisoned', 'Disappeared', 'International law violated'. There are photographs of dead and missing children. The details? Here is just one example. A former political prisoner who was detained for five months at al-Karkh Security Directorate in April 1985 spoke to Amnesty after his release about how his own family were tortured in front of his eyes to make him confess. He said: '[My] mother [seventy-three years old], three sisters and three brothers, with five children aged between five and thirteen, were arrested and brought in front of me. They were subjected to the falaqa [beatings on the soles of the feet] and electric shocks . . .'

The Amnesty pamphlet continues: 'His testimony also described conditions under which infants have been held in some Iraqi prisons: "Usually they keep such children in a separate cell next to the mother's or father's cell and deprive them of milk in order to force the parents to confess. I saw a five-month-old baby screaming in this state."'

The MPs were extremely busy in the run-up to the Christmas break. Hugh Dykes said on 18 December 1992: 'Sorry. Can't help you with that. I just don't have the time. Good luck with the book.'

Old Harrovian Tony Nelson, now a government minister at the Treasury, did not file the 1989 trip in the 1990 edition of the *Register of Members' Interests*. A message was left with Tony Nelson's secretary at the House of Commons on 14 December 1992, and again the following day. The secretary said: 'Oh, yes, you rang yesterday. The message is probably taking a long time to filter through because he's in the Treasury, now, did you know?' A flurry of further calls to HM Treasury met with the eventual response from a government press officer, Adam Linford, that Nelson filed the trip in the 1991 edition of the *Register*.

Nelson is described in Roth's *Parliamentary Profiles* as a 'mason'. You may recall that, in 1974, after Saddam's secret police had discovered the guest list of a masonic party held in 1942, they arrested and executed the 'Masonic plotters', including the oldest victim aged ninety-two. N. Safwat in *Freemasonry in the Arab World* (London: Arab Research Centre, 1980) cites the Iraqi law on freemasonry: 'Whoever promotes Zionist principles, including Freemasonry, or belongs to any of its institutions, or helps them materially or morally, or works in any form for achieving its purposes shall be executed.' It is therefore unlikely that Nelson informed his hosts that he was 'on the square'.

Timothy Smith, another Old Harrovian, was telephoned on 14 December 1992 and a message was left with his secretary. The following day he was telephoned again and a second message was left with his secretary. She told researcher Alice Pitman to phone back between three and four o'clock that afternoon. Alice phoned at the requested time. The MP was too busy. Alice asked whether Smith could ring her. The secretary said she would pass the message on but thought that this was unlikely. On 17 December 1992, another message was left with the switchboard.

Timothy Wood was telephoned on 14 December 1992, a message was left, and again the next day – and yet again on the next. On 17 December 1992, his secretary said: 'He's terribly tied up at the moment, it's the last day, but I'll try and get something out of him and get back to you.' Wood is described in Roth's *Parliamentary Profiles* as a 'free-tripper to the Arab world'. After the trip to Iraq, he visited Morocco as guest of its government in January 1990 and he visited Jordan and the West Bank at the invitation of the Bow Group in April 1990.

Nicolas Bennett is no longer in the House of Commons.

By coincidence, someone else important to this story was a guest of the Iraqis, but not free to leave. On 15 September 1989, some days before the MPs flew to Baghdad, the secret police had arrested a British journalist and an *Observer* colleague at Saddam Hussein International Airport. According to Dr al-Hassan, the MPs flew back to London, as they had arrived, on Iraqi Airways. While Bennett, Dykes, Marlow, Nelson, Smith and Wood were enjoying Iraqi hospitality, Saddam's men started the slow torture of Farzad Bazoft.

CHAPTER
EIGHT

Farzad had charm to burn. I didn't know him very well, having joined the *Observer* only a few months before his arrest. But I remember one occasion – it must have been in the summer of 1989 – at the coffee machine in what some like to call 'the whited sepulchre' of the *Observer* office in Battersea. We both arrived at the coffee machine at the same time and he stood back and waved me forward with a punctilio that was sent up by his eyes. It was a banal, everyday thing, but Farzad carried it off with such comedy that it fixed in my mind. That is the last time I can recall seeing him.

What happened after his arrest can be deduced from the eyewitness account of his friend, Dee (Daphne Ann) Parish, retold in *Prisoner in Baghdad*, written with Pat Lancaster (London: Chapmans, 1992).

He was blindfold. I gasped to see how thin he was, but it was him, unmistakably. His hair, his mouth, his hands, the way he stood, I was in no doubt this wasn't a trick. Farzad was here in prison, but still it made no sense. I stared at his thin frame in the baggy prison-issue pyjamas and remembered how, only a few short weeks ago, he had looked so healthy and handsome in blue jeans and a pale blue shirt as we set off for Hilla. As I continued to stare he was bundled away, looking more like a broken old man than the witty, vital friend with whom I had enjoyed so much laughter and good conversation.

As Farzad left the room, the Iraqi football match [on the television] was switched off and a video cartridge was loaded into a machine. Suddenly, Farzad's face filled the screen. Beneath his eyes there were deep, black shadows as he stared vacantly out of the set. I had never seen Farzad looking like this; he must have suffered dreadfully, I thought. But as he began to speak, his words seemed to contradict my impressions.

'The treatment I have received', he gulped, blinking his eyes rapidly, 'is much better than I would receive in a detention centre or institution in the UK.' He went on: 'In 1983 I got to know some Israeli intelligence officers as friends and in 1987 I was recruited by Israeli intelligence agents living in the United Kingdom under different covers.'

I listened in horror as his confession continued. He began to talk about the ill-fated trip to the explosion site at Hilla . . . There was no reason Farzad would say the things he was saying unless he had been forced to make a speech written by the interrogators. It was the only explanation.

We watched the video of Farzad's confession in the office on 1 November 1989. I remember the sickening silence once Donald Trelford, the editor, switched the video off. There was a terrible feeling of helplessness.

Farzad had gone to Baghdad with a number of other international journalists, invited by the Iraqis to cover the Baathists' version of democratic elections in Kurdistan in early September 1989. He was a freelance, working 'on spec', meaning that the paper was interested but not committed to running anything he might write. It was his decision to go. After the end of the Iran-Iraq war, news interest in the area was dimming. Because he was going, just like the MPs, as a guest of the Iraqi government there was no obvious worry about his safety. He had been to Iraq five times before.

The day he left for Iraq a much better story than the stooge elections broke on the front page of the *Independent*: 'Huge explosion at secret Iraqi missile plant: Egyptian technicians among about 700 killed in disaster near Baghdad.' The story was dated 6 September 1989, but the explosion at the huge al-Iskanderia military complex near Hilla, south of Baghdad on the road to Babylon, was believed to have happened on 17 August 1989. The story broke not in Baghdad – the Mukhabarat saw to that – but in Egypt, where base staff at al-Mazha airport reported seeing one plane unload only military coffins, and doctors and nurses specializing in skin grafts and burns drafted in to the Maadi military hospital. It had been a big bang. According to Kenneth Timmerman – who knows about these things – 'the explosion momentarily blinded the NSA's [the National Security Agency of the United States] KH-II Keyhole satellite when it passed over Iraq several hours later.'

Rumours buzzed around Baghdad that the explosion had been one of Saddam's chemical warfare factories blowing up. They were fortified by the descriptions of the burns coming out of Egypt. It now seems that the explosion was not poison gas but rocket fuel going up at the al-Qaqa missile plant within the al-Iskanderia military complex, where Egyptian military advisers (and Argentinians) were working on a rocket that would put the first Iraqi weapon into space. The al-Qaqa plant was run by the Iraqi Ministry of Industry and Military Industrialization. Just down the road was 'the Hutteen General Establishment for Mechanical Industries in Iskandria', cited in the 30 November 1987 MI5 report as an end user of Matrix Churchill lathes.

The world's media at the time had no certainty about what had happened. The journalists decided that the only way to square the contradictory reports was to see for themselves. A television news crew from ITN, a crew from Dutch television and others all streamed down the Babylon road. One group was stopped and detained by security forces, but was later released as they had got nowhere near the site. Another journalist hired a taxi and drove south, but when the cabbie realized the purpose of the fare 'he went white with fear' and did a U-turn. Farzad heard about the failed attempts and figured out how he could get to the site without being stopped. He was, after all, from the London *Observer*, not the *Baghdad Court Circular*.

Farzad made no secret of his plans to visit the site, even asking the deputy foreign minister for his permission to go. He asked officials in the Iraqi Foreign Office if they could lay on a driver. They said they would do their best, but nothing came of it. Next, he turned to Dee Parish who was working at the Irish Hospital in Baghdad. He charmed her into driving down to Hilla in a hospital car, she in a uniform, he dressed up as an Indian doctor. Being Iranian, he looked the part. (His nationality had never been a probem in Iraq because Farzad was an anti-Ayatollah Iranian. Baghdad was full of Iranian exiles, some of whom fought with the Iraqis against Iran.)

Pretending to be a doctor may seem a dubious device for a journalist to employ in a British context, but Iraq was Iraq. He was not the first journalist to do so while struggling to uncover the truth in a totalitarian state that year. In June 1989, while filming wards choked with the victims of the Tiananmen Square massacre in Peking, hospital staff put a doctor's coat on the BBC's Kate Adie to hide her from the Chinese secret police.

Farzad's courage paid off. He took photographs, samples of soil, a damaged shoe and some tattered clothing. His logic was simple: he planned to repeat Gwynne Roberts's feat in Kurdistan of bringing back to Britain forensic evidence which would establish the cause of the explosion. It was a scoop which would make his name and land him a salaried job on the paper, his goal.

He went to the British embassy and asked an official if the embassy would ship his samples from the explosion to Britain. (Mark Higson, then the Iraqi desk officer at the Foreign Office, confirms Farzad's approach.) This, too, sounds unusual, but embassies sometimes bend the rules. This time they did not. Lending assistance to exhibitors at the 1989 Baghdad military exhibition was one thing; helping a journalist find out why one of Saddam's weapons factories had blown up was quite another. Farzad would have to carry out his soil samples himself. Later, some MPs and others claimed, without furnishing any evidence, that Farzad was a spy. They should have stopped to think. Had he been a spy, it would have been logical for his agency to ship out the samples themselves rather than risk losing them to the Iraqis. The British, American, Chinese, Soviet, West and East Europeans all had functioning embassies in Baghdad. One can also safely assume that the Israelis and the Iranians would have ways of getting things safely out of Baghdad, for example, via the Kurds, the Shias or Middle-Eastern businessmen. That Farzad had to take out the soil samples himself is the strongest possible argument that he was not a spy, but what he said he was: a reporter.

But the soil samples, evidence of his innocence on the spying charge, were to be his doom. It meant that when the Mukhabarat (or one of the other fifty-seven varieties of secret policemen) stopped him at the airport, he knew that all they had to do was to take a quick look inside his bag and he was in trouble.

He lasted four days before they came for Dee Parish. If readers care to remember the thirty different forms of torture used by the Iraqis, those ninety-six hours may well represent a heroic attempt to protect his friend. He broke around the time the Iraqi Airways jet touched down at Saddam Hussein International Airport with Marlow's delegation of fact-finding British MPs on board.

The story appeared in London papers on 22 September 1989, but Dr al-Hassan recalled: 'We arrived in Iraq on 19 September. We knew about the arrest of Farzad Bazoft while we were there.' Did the MPs campaign as a delegation for the immediate release of Farzad Bazoft with the Iraqis? He replied: 'The case was very new. It was not in their itinerary to raise that problem. No one knew what was happening.'

Farzad's arrest was a major inconvenience to the sweet course of Anglo-Iraq trade. Ministers in parliamentary answers stressed that there were two Britons in Iraqi prisons: Mrs Parish and Ian Richter. Farzad Bazoft, they reminded MPs, was an Iranian national travelling on British papers. It was a fine distinction, but one which was not lost in Baghdad. Of course, the Foreign Office and Major himself wanted all three safe and home and civil servants like Mark Higson worked hard to achieve that. But from Farzad's arrest onwards, Whitehall sent out a set

of conflicting signals to Saddam. The public signals all sema-
phored the anxiety of the British government to see the three
prisoners released; the confidential signals showed them to be
expendable pawns.

Very much in public the new foreign secretary John Major
went to New York to get the measure of the United Nations.
There he met his Iraqi opposite number, Tareq Aziz, pressed
him to release the three prisoners and complained that Britain
had not been allowed consular access to Farzad.

Major was briefed before the meeting on 29 September 1989.
It would be reasonable to assume that the briefing contained
references to other features of the Anglo-Iraq relationship, such
as Foreign Office concerns that the government had 'firm evidence' that Matrix Churchill machine tools were being used to
enhance Iraqi military capability and wider worries about the
Iraqi procurement network which had so exercised Major's
junior minister, William Waldegrave, that summer.

Moreover, as foreign secretary, Major would naturally be
sent the juiciest MI6 intelligence. A secret document from the
Matrix Churchill file, dated 5 September 1989 but giving the
date of the information received as 1 September 1989, stated:

> Dr Fadel Kadhum, an Iraqi procurement official in the UK,
> said that his company TDG bought a share in the Learfan
> factory to obtain access to carbon-fibre technology. [Handy if
> you want to build rockets.] Dr Kadhum, who is a legal adviser
> to the Iraqi Ministry of Military Industrialization, was angry
> at the government refusal of HMG to provide grants for the
> reopening of the factory. He did not reveal Iraq's response to
> the refusal . . .

Was the foreign secretary made aware by MI6 that the
Iraqis had a grudge against Britain – a grudge they might, for
example, act on by seizing an intrepid reporter and torturing
him to confess that he was a spy? If that was the case, Farzad
was taken because he was from Britain, not Iran.

Challenged by Labour's trade and industry spokesman,

Robin Cook, on the contents of the pre-Aziz meeting briefing Major was stung into writing back the very same day – Saturday 14 November 1992. Major did not touch on what secret information he had seen. But he did confirm that in the briefing paper there was 'reference to Matrix Churchill (and Learfan) [which] was an example of British media interest in Iraqi procurement activities in the UK'.

Earlier in 1992, Major released the document entitled 'Questions of procedure for ministers' in which he said that ministers had a 'duty to give Parliament and the public as full information as possible about the policies, decisions and actions of the government'.

This trumpet call for open government did not extend to Major's briefing papers, when foreign secretary, on Anglo-Iraq relations prior to meeting Tareq Aziz, because he gave no further clue as to what, precisely, he meant by 'an example of British media interest in Iraqi procurement activities in the UK' which referred to Learfan and Matrix Churchill. However, those references provide a useful clue which narrows down the possible candidates. There were four articles in September 1989, which touched on both Matrix Churchill and Learfan, three in the *Financial Times* and one in the *Observer*. If Major glanced at any one of them, he would have been immediately alerted to the fears of the British Foreign Office (where he worked, remember, as foreign secretary) that Matrix Churchill technology was arming Iraq.

The three articles in the *Financial Times* are headlined 'Matrix confirms it exhibited at Baghdad arms fair', dated 13 September 1989, 'Iraqi military buying "financed by unauthorized BNL credits"', dated 20 September 1989, and a half-page spread, featuring three stories headlined 'Network of companies with Baghdad ties', 'The short step from harmless machinery to lethal arms technology' and 'Italians begin to ponder armaments link in sales', dated 21 September 1989. A flow chart on the *Financial Times* half-page was well appreciated throughout Whitehall as a handy reference. The Foreign Office civil servant David Gore-Booth minuted on 31 October 1989: 'Lord Trefgarne's astonishing claim that Matrix Churchill is somehow separate from Iraqi arms procurement activities / Learfan can be exploded by showing him the nice diagram in the *FT* of 21 September which demonstrates the organic connection!'

The *Observer* article, dated 3 September 1989, is of the four contenders perhaps the most likely one to have been in Major's red box. Headlined 'Iraq-linked firm buys defence factory' it was an Alan George exclusive breaking the news of the Foreign Office fears about the Iraqi takeover at the Belfast factory Learfan. Illustrated with a picture of Saddam, the article is an extremely well-informed piece on Learfan, Matrix Churchill, Dr Bull's SRC outfit and the various Baghdad connections. George wrote:

> The Belfast project is not the first British investment of the Iraqi-directed TDG, raising fears in Whitehall that Baghdad may be involved in a systematic programme to acquire British technology with defence applications.
>
> In 1987 the company, operating through a related firm, TMG Engineering Ltd, gained 92.5 per cent control of Coventry-based Matrix Churchill Ltd, the UK's leading producer of computer-controlled machine tools.

There are three reasons for suspecting that this Alan George story in the *Observer* was the one in Major's box: first, it gave prominent place to Learfan; second, it was a fine summary of Foreign Office fears about the Iraqis; third, the article itself. It set off a chain reaction of other stories on the Iraqi arms procurement network in the *Financial Times* and the *Daily Telegraph*. The Iraqis would not have liked it one bit. The 3 September 1989 article touched on a possible motive for the Iraqis to be nasty to the British – something MI6 knew three days before – that the Iraqi procurement lawyer, Dr Kudhum, was 'angry' about the British government's refusal to throw money at the new Baghdad-backed Learfan factory. The denial of aid to Learfan could have been the reason why they wanted revenge – and Farzad walked into a trap from which all the charm in the world could not extract him.

But a brief skimming of any of the four stories that contain the magic words 'Matrix Churchill' and 'Learfan' would appear to sit awkwardly with Major's statement in a letter to Labour MP Tam Dalyell, on 23 November 1992, that he saw a minute referring to Matrix Churchill after the invasion of Kuwait. Major wrote:

> I first became aware of the investigation into Matrix Churchill in October 1990 . . . At the beginning of August 1990, following the invasion of Kuwait, I did see a copy of a minute about the implications of the invasion for trade with Iraq. That minute referred to Matrix Churchill as one company with potential exports that would need to be prevented.

But look carefully at the economy with which Major (or the Cabinet Office functionaries) drafted the letter. 'I first became aware of the investigation into Matrix Churchill in October 1990 . . .'

Consider: the 'investigation' which led to charges against the Matrix Churchill Three is one thing; the Foreign Office fears that Matrix Churchill machine tools were arming Iraq quite another. When did Major 'first become aware' of those fears involving Matrix Churchill? The letter does not say. It volunteers from Major that: 'following the invasion of Kuwait, I did see a copy of a minute about the implications of the invasion for trade with Iraq. That minute referred to Matrix Churchill . . .' The implicit sense appears to be that he 'first became aware' of Matrix Churchill 'following the invasion of Kuwait' but that is a false reading. There is no mention of the 'first became aware' formula on the particular matter of the fears about Matrix Churchill – as opposed to the Customs investigation into it. The 23 November 1992 letter to Tam Dalyell is so economically worded that it does square with his 14 November 1992 letter to Robin Cook in which he confirmed that in the briefing paper for the Tareq Aziz meeting in New York there was 'reference to Matrix Churchill (and Learfan) [which] was an example of British media interest in Iraqi procurement activities in the UK'. One can only admire the quality in the drafting of both letters, an exquisite refinement of the art of telling the truth.

The purpose of going into this close textual analysis is that first, Major, prior to his meeting with the Iraqi foreign minister in September 1989, had in his briefing papers a newspaper story about fears of Iraqi arms procurement, Matrix Churchill and Learfan. Second, the Foreign Office fear that the newspaper story itself may have angered the Iraqis meant that it was not peripheral but a key document in that briefing. Major ought to have read it; his civil servants ought to have brought it to his attention. Third, he has yet to tell the House of Commons when he first became aware of the Foreign Office fears about Matrix Churchill and the Iraqi procurement network.

We now come to an omission. Absence of evidence is evidence of absence. Nowhere in the entire Matrix Churchill document paper chase, the hundreds of press cuttings, Hansard speeches and lengthy conversations with some of the key players in the Iraqgate scandal is there a mention that the British government considered threatening to stop the secret trade with Iraq to spring the British prisoners, or better, hostages, held in Baghdad: Farzad, Mrs Parish and Ian Richter. It did not appear to be an option. Major appealed to the Iraqis for clemency in New York, but there is no evidence that those appeals were backed with muscle – as a London cabbie would say, 'the only language that Saddam would understand'.

The hostages did not appear to be uppermost in the minds of the DTI. Lord Trefgarne, who had been switched to the DTI and was now minister for trade, wrote to Waldegrave on 5 October 1989 calling for the Howe guidelines to be scrapped completely. He wrote that the arguments for revoking licences had 'weakened to the point of extinction'. He added that 'the Learfan affair did not involve Matrix Churchill' and that he was 'not aware of any evidence to challenge the company's assurance that there is no

Iraqi involvement in the management of Matrix Churchill itself', points at which Gore-Booth sneered when he raised the 'nice diagram' in the *Financial Times* on the Iraqi procurement network.

If you don't like a regime, you boycott it. Kurt Waldheim, the president of Austria, suffered an almost total boycott by foreign heads of state because of suspicions that he knew about the Holocaust while an intelligence officer in the German army during Hitler's War. If you condemn a tyranny as 'barbaric' for its use of poison gas against innocents, plead for clemency on behalf of your own imprisoned citizens, but keep on sending and receiving ministers to and from the tyranny to promote trade, then the strong man is free to deduce that the condemnations are froth, not substance.

Consider. While Major was foreign secretary all the plans for the next meeting of the Anglo-Iraq joint trade commission, to take place in London from 27 to 30 November 1989, were firmed up. It was Trefgarne's turn to host the celebration of common commercial interests. Mohammed Mehdi Saleh represented the Iraqi side.

Consider, too, the visit of Cabinet Energy Secretary and Old Carthusian John Wakeham to Baghdad from 12 to 15 October 1989. As foreign secretary, Major must have been aware of the diplomatic benefit to Saddam of a British Cabinet minister arriving in Baghdad, giving the regime a desperately needed fresh coat of respect, or, better, varnish. The *Baghdad Observer* was positively ecstatic: 'Iraq and Britain hold joint seminar on oil, gas industry' was the headline on 15 October 1989. The newspaper reported:

> Around 80 British experts from the British departments of Trade and Industry and Energy, major British oil companies and around 300 Iraqi oil experts are taking part in a three day seminar ...
>
> In an interview with the *Baghdad Observer* the British Secretary of State for Energy said: 'I am the first Cabinet minister to visit Iraq since the (Iran-Iraq) ceasefire. [This was not correct. Tony Newton was a Cabinet minister, though

serving under Lord Young, when he went to Baghdad as trade minister in 1988.] This emphasizes Britain's belief in continuing good relations with Iraq. I would also like to take this opportunity to stress the political importance which the British government attaches to a further strengthening of British-Iraq relations.'

And the March 1989 Amnesty International report on the five-month-old baby screaming for food in the next cell, to make its mother confess? British 'revulsion' at Iraq 'barbarities'? The appeals for clemency? The *Baghdad Observer* made no mention of these. There is, however, a photograph of Wakeham in a suit, his hands folded: an icon of smooth satisfaction.

The *Baghdad Observer* reported on Wakeham meeting Brigadier Hussein Kamil Majid and foreign minister Tareq Aziz. The paper listed some of the British companies in Baghdad for the seminar: BP, British Gas, British Steel, John Crane, Rolls-Royce, BICC Cables, Babcock. It quoted Iain Millar of the DTI: 'Iraq is a nation which has abundant oil reserves, so we can mutually benefit from the use of modern technology and expertise offered by British know-how.'

One of the oilmen went to the bunfight at the al-Rashid hotel, thrown by the British for their Iraqi hosts. 'Wakeham? We called him Sleepham. The general attitude of the British government party was that Farzad was an embuggerance (*sic*). I remember one of the party – not Wakeham – saying that it was ridiculous to dress up as an Indian doctor. They certainly didn't protest to the Iraqis about it in my presence.'

Wakeham did ask Aziz about Farzad and Dee Parish, according to a report in the *Independent* on 16 October 1989. The Cabinet minister was told that though no charges had been pressed, the nature of the case against the two was 'espionage'. Wakeham may well have pressed the Iraqis very hard to release the three in prison, but he did not succeed. The government's difficulty was that, because it was committed to trading with Iraq, it was trapped into playing the 'constant hostage game', an entertainment played on Saddam's terms. Once again, the game stopped with the Iraqis holding all the chips.

A few days after Wakeham came home, chancellor Nigel Lawson quit, and on 26 October 1989 Mrs Thatcher switched Major from the Foreign Office to the Treasury. Douglas Hurd added one more Old Etonian to the Foreign Office's tally.

The following day, British intelligence reported the first evidence of Dr Bull's supergun project in Britain. Blueprints of the amazing projectile had been provided by Paul Henderson, who throughout this period had been visiting Iraq. The secret minutes recorded that Henderson 'gave us the attached blueprints. This [projectile] could have a range of 1,200 km: it could be connected with the Space Research Corporation's involvement with long-range artillery research.'

The supergun is the biggest red herring in the Iraqgate affair, one which fixated the attentions of the Trade and Industry Select Committee to the exclusion of much else. But as the former MI6 agent and writer on intelligence matters James Rusbridger has pointed out, the supergun was always a nonsense. A supergun was a fitting toy for a tyrant, but it went against all military logic. At best, it could be fired once: then the spy satellites would locate it instantly, and blow it to kingdom come.

There is no doubting that the intelligence community in Whitehall were grateful for Henderson's co-operation. There is no doubting his courage in returning to Baghdad throughout this period right up to the invasion. However, information – especially secret information – is never cost-free. MI6 received information; the Iraqis got British technology in their weapons factories, plus a London base for their arms procurement network. The question that government ministers never appeared to address is, who was getting the best out of the exchange: Britain or Iraq? From Henderson, MI6 would have got a necessarily compartmentalized insight into Iraq's war machine, but – no fault of the agent – very little on Saddam's real purposes, intentions and future plans. We now know those future plans included an invasion of a nation state with historic and vital strategic ties to Britain. As Whitehall's spies too were distracted by the supergun puzzle, they missed the big one. Saddam, it seems, won the poker game with MI6 too.

Three events central to our story crowded in on 1 November 1989. First, the opening of the 1989 Baghdad trade fair. At the US pavilion there was a written welcome from President George Bush. The DTI were pushing the British pavilion, hosting seventy UK companies. Second, the video of Farzad's 'confession' was shown on Iraq TV and picked up and screened in Britain. The drugged face, his eyes blinking like Gatling guns, parts of his moustache gone, as if they had been plucked out, the voice of another man, seemingly checking off Farzad's robotic account . . . Another victim of Saddam's torture. And, third, three British ministers agreed to send yet more Matrix Churchill machine tools to Iraq, despite the evidence that they were going to arm Saddam. Clark, Trefgarne and Waldegrave met at Trefgarne's office at the House of Lords at 4 p.m. on 1 November 1989. A Foreign Office minute, dated 6 November 1989, sums up the argument: Waldegrave

> repeated his concerns about Iraqi involvement in CW [chemical warfare] production, missile development and possible nuclear weapons research . . . He remained very concerned that Matrix Churchill was part of an Iraqi procurement network in the UK. It was incorrect to claim as Lord Trefgarne had done, that the Iraqis had no say in the management of the company: Matrix Churchill was 95 per cent Iraqi-owned.

Clark and Trefgarne argued that the war between Iraq and Iran was over, and because of that the guidelines should be scrapped. Waldegrave 'replied that the defence sales guidelines were government policy, and could not be lifted at the level of this meeting'. But he conceded ground on all four applications by Matrix Churchill to have their machine tools licensed, provided that 'any Parliamentary Questions or public condemnation arising from the issue of licences should be dealt with by the DTI'.

None of the summaries of the meeting refer to the Kurds, the Amnesty reports, the three hostages held in Baghdad, the evidence that Iraq was a poor financial risk.

It was an ignoble hour.

On 10 November 1989 Mrs Thatcher told the House of Commons: 'Supplies of British defence equipment to Iraq and Iran continue to be governed by the guidelines introduced in 1985.' In the light of the unannounced change to the Howe guidelines in 1988, the prime minister's statement was . . . well, make up your own mind.

Habobi, living cosily in the Matrix Churchill company flat in Hampstead, and Dr Kadhum soon learned the good news from Matrix Churchill and, no doubt, passed it on to Baghdad. Saddam realized that he could get away with murder. And this is what he proceeded to do.

> Robin [Kealy, first secretary at the British Embassy in Baghdad] looked pale and strained as he leaned towards me across the coffee table. 'Dee [Parish],' he said quietly, 'the news is not good. Farzad was executed this morning.'
>
> I blinked at him. The whole of my body went into shock. All sense of feeling left my arms and legs so that it seemed just my whirling head was suspended in space.
>
> 'Oh, no,' I whispered. 'Oh, no, no, no . . .'

The trial of Farzad and Dee Parish, according to the account in her book, had been a joke, a gabble in Arabic in front of two people who did not have the language. The death sentence on Farzad Bazoft had been passed a few days before, to international protests from writers, newspapers, governments around the world. But some were not very bothered, either before or after his state-sanctioned murder.

The night before he was hanged on 15 March 1990, Sarah, Duchess of York burst into a dinner party held at Le Gavroche by the then honorary treasurer of the Conservative Party, Lord McAlpine – educated at Stowe public school – with two men in tow, neither of them the Duke. One was Steve Wyatt, son of the Texan oilman, Oscar Wyatt, whose Coastal Petroleum did a huge amount of business with Iraq. The second was Dr Ramzi Salman, the then head of the Iraqi State Oil Marketing Organization, now Saddam's voice on OPEC, the Organization of Petroleum Exporting Countries.

Dr Salman had been reportedly wined and dined in the Duchess's private apartment at Buckingham Palace, a breach of protocol for which the Duchess was reportedly reproached. The tabloids got hold of the story of the two strings to the Duchess's bow, but got very excited at a remark by Steve Wyatt. 'Mah woman and I sit together', reported the *Daily Mirror* on 17 January 1992, adding in italics: 'Oily Texan sticks close to Fergie at posh dinner'. Wyatt's thick Texan accent may have caused a mishearing: one of the diners suspected that he could have said, 'Ma'am and I sit together.' But the diner, though not wishing to be named, was quietly angry with the Duchess for the *faux pas*: 'It was insensitive and stupid of her having the Iraqi there, given the case of the *Observer* journalist.'

Dr Salman would, no doubt, have appreciated the invitation to Buckingham Palace, a nice social titbit to bring back to Baghdad. Steve Wyatt was, no doubt, happy that a distinguished and valued business partner of his father had been so royally treated. Two months after Farzad was hanged the Duchess was the Wyatts' guest at a villa complex in Morocco called La Gazelle d'Or, near Taroudant, described by the French baron who used to own it as the 'most romantic holiday location on earth'. She has also enjoyed the hospitality of the Wyatts at their palatial villa in Cap Ferrat in the south of France and their opulent home, Allington, in Houston, Texas.

There is no mention of the Duchess in the Matrix Churchill secret documents. But consider the following evidence.

Dr Salman was head of the State Oil Marketing Organization of Iraq. The State Oil Marketing Organization of Iraq is named in a letter, dated 1 November 1990, by British civil servant Paul St J. Miller to another civil servant at the ECGD (for which the then Chief Secretary Norman Lamont was the responsible Treasury minister). Miller's letter was headed: 'Matrix Churchill: Industrias Cardoen Ltda – Chile'. He wrote:

> You may be interested to learn that Cardoen would be paid by the Iraqi's [*sic*] in local currency and then use that currency, with Iraqi government authority, to purchase crude oil from the State Oil Marketing Organization of Iraq . . . Thus, the Iraqi's [*sic*] do not use vital hard currency and US dollars are ultimately received by Cardoen via the oil trader from proceeds generated by what was in effect a barter deal.

Earlier in the letter, Miller set out the apparent previous character of the business between Matrix Churchill and Cardoen: 'Goods were apparently destined for Iraq to be incorporated into a chemical weapons factory.' Miller is, in fact, summarizing the contents of the 24 August 1989 'crown jewels' when ECGD civil servant S. Matthews stated that the government had approved insurance cover for £4 million and noted that the 'goods were destined for Iraq, to be incorporated into a chemical weapons factory'. The approval decision was taken on 15 March 1989, when Major was the Treasury minister responsible for export credits.

According to one knowledgeable Iraqi exile, Dr Salman, the Duchess's Iraqi friend, is thick with Saddam. Being a senior player in the Baathist regime, he would be under no illusions about Iraq's use of violence and poison gas as weapons of political control. *Vanity Fair* magazine dedicated a long section of its April 1991 profile of the head of the Wyatt family, Oscar, to the close links between Oscar and Saddam and another section to the links between the Duchess and the Wyatts.

By inviting Dr Salman to Buckingham Palace, the Duchess signalled that senior Iraqi players were, despite everything, welcome at the Palace. By going out on the town with Dr Salman, the Duchess endowed social respectability on the Iraqis.

The Duchess may not have heard of Halabja, would not have read of the reference made by a British civil servant to the

State Oil Marketing Organization of Iraq and the goods 'to be incorporated into a chemical weapons factory' in the same letter. For her future benefit, then, a cutting on chemical weapons, from the *Observer*, dated 17 March 1991: reporter Julie Flint interviewed one of the victims of Halabja, who told her this story of how she tried to care for a gas victim, a boy. He was six years old.

> 'Chemical was coming out of his body like water, dripping from him to my mother's head. There was a very, very bad smell. He·died in my arms, shaking his body. I held his hand, but his heart was not beating . . . [Later] a young man ran up . . . He was crying and shouting: "Oh my God . . ." I said: "Sorry, I think this is your son," and gave him his dead son.'

The government used the same language in public for Farzad as they had for Halabja. In the House of Commons Mrs Thatcher said of Farzad's hanging: 'This is an act of barbarism, deeply repugnant to all civilized people.' Hurd said: 'By their action, the Iraqi authorities have blackened the name of the Iraq across the world,' adding that Britain had been foremost in making representations about Iraq's record on poisonous gases and human rights.

That was for public consumption. So was this, though not to be sourced back to the government: 'HANGED MAN WAS A ROBBER' screamed the *Sun* front page, on 16 March 1990. The *Sun* made much of the Iraqis' callousness, including a quotation from 'gloating Iraqi information minister Latif Nassayif Jassim' – whom the British MPs had met in 1988 – 'Thatcher wanted him alive . . . we sent him in a box.' But equally callous was the decision to leak to newspapers like the *Sun* details of Farzad's criminal conviction for a sad and bungled robbery in August 1981 in which no one was hurt. Pauline Ingleby, the building society clerk who had been held up by Farzad, had nothing but pity for the hanged man: 'To be honest, the robbery had no lasting effect on me. In fact, I was more shocked to discover that the man had been hanged in Iraq. I felt very sorry for him. I was horrified,' she told the *Daily Mirror* on 17 March 1990. The leak did not come from the building society. The *Sun*'s Simon Walters wrote: 'The British newsman hanged in Iraq yesterday was a convicted robber, a security source revealed last night.' 'Security source' means a government spokesman. It was defensive briefing with a vengeance. The British government, mindful of the value of Anglo-Iraq trade, were furiously discounting the integrity of Saddam's latest victim.

There was worse to come.

Terry Dicks, the Conservative MP for Hayes and Harlington, said he would ask questions about Farzad's criminal record. The *Daily Telegraph* quoted Dicks on 17 March 1990: 'I want to know why this stateless person was not deported. He should have been booted out.' The *Daily Telegraph* went on to report: 'The Foreign Office and the Home Office strenuously denied that they tried to smear Mr Bazoft by disclosing his conviction to fend off demands for tougher action against Iraq.' The *Daily Telegraph* did not mention in its report that Dicks had filed in the *Parliamentary Register of Members' Interest* that he had visited Iraq from 25 September to 2 October 1988, as a 'guest of Iraqi government'. Asked about his trip to Iraq, Dicks replied: 'No thanks. I'm not interested.'

In the same *Daily Telegraph* report, the newspaper revealed:

> In reply to a question from Mr Tim Smith, Tory MP for Beaconsfield, Mr Hurd said on Thursday that Mr Bazoft had telephoned Scotland Yard four times 'as a member of the public offering information on subject unconnected with Iraq'.
>
> Mr Smith is understood to have been asked by the government to raise the question so that rumours of Special Branch involvement could be dispelled.

That is artful. Far from dispelling 'rumours', Hurd's part-confirmation of the story that Farzad spoke to the Special Branch on a few occasions also helped to tarnish his integrity beyond the grave. The *Telegraph* report did not mention that Smith had filed a trip to Iraq in the *Register of Members' Interests* or that Smith visited Iraq while Farzad was also a guest of the Iraqis, though under more unpleasant circumstances. The following day the *Daily Mail* announced that Smith had resigned his chairmanship of the Commons Anglo-Iraq group.

Hurd also announced that the British ambassador to Baghdad was to be recalled, but diplomatic ties would not be broken. Nor would the £250 million trade credits agreed last November be cancelled. The *Independent* on 16 March 1990 quoted an anonymous Conservative MP: 'I came to the House thinking politics was about ideas. Politics is about money. You decide about the money, and then make the ideas fit.'

Another Conservative MP, Rupert Allason, alleged that Farzad was 'probably' an Israeli spy. The *Observer*'s editor, Donald Trelford, countered: 'If Mr Allason has a single scrap of evidence that Farzad spied for anyone, let him produce it.' Allason did not.

But the damage was done to Farzad's good name. It was only after the invasion of Kuwait that some in Fleet Street and Westminster might have had occasion to wonder whether they had judged the reporter on the trail of a scoop too harshly.

Jonathan Moyle was the next journalist to die investigating Iraq's arms procurement network. The editor of *Defence Helicopter World*, he was found dead in Room 1406 at the Carrera Hotel, Santiago, Chile on 31 March 1990. He was 28, a former helicopter pilot with the RAF and engaged to be married in two months. A hotel maid, Sylvia Cabrera, found him hanging by the neck by one of his own shirts from a rail in a clothes cupboard in his bedroom, naked except for a plastic bag around his head and, according to Peter Ford in the *Independent*, 9 June 1990, 'an improvised nappy made from a towel and a polythene bag over two pairs of underpants.'

In the days after his death the Chilean police found that Moyle had committed suicide. Gossip at the British embassy added a sexual angle to the 'suicide' theory. Ford reported: 'According to Chilean investigators, the first time the "death while masturbating" theory surfaced was on 31 May 1990 at a British embassy reception for the visiting Archbishop of

Canterbury . . . British intelligence officials are reliably said to have offered the same version of Moyle's death in a briefing to [selected] journalists in London on the same day.'

The effect of the gossip and the intelligence briefing was to dampen journalists' interest in the case. Moyle's father, Tony, a retired mathematics teacher who lives in Devon, his mother, Diana, and his fiancée, Dr Annette Kissenbeck, were grief-stricken. They could not believe the suicide theory, and were shocked and sickened by the 'sexual' angle. But the evidence of the 'nappy' – rehearsed at the British embassy in Chile and by British intelligence – pointed to an unhappy suicide, not murder.

Unless, that is, you happen to know that wrapping your victim in a 'nappy' is a trick of the trade of the professional hitman. BBC2's *Newsnight* reported on 3 December 1991: 'The bag over the head had helped to suffocate him and to prevent the smell of any subsequent vomit; the nappy to prevent the smell of any subsequent defecation, thus allowing the killer time to escape, leaving the body hanging undetected for as long as possible.'

Once you study the precise details of the Moyle killing, the suicide theory looks less and less likely.

Moyle was in Chile to attend an arms fair and to investigate Carlos Cardoen's cannibalizing of Western technology for the Iraqis, including refashioning American Bell helicopters and British 'smart' anti-ship mines. He may too have been interested in the precise end-use of the Matrix Churchill machine tools which were delivered to an Iraqi munitions factory, via Cardoen. Western intelligence believed the Iraqis were making chemical weapons at a Cardoen munitions factory, as the *Financial Times* reported in 1988.

Three days before his death nuclear bomb triggers destined for Iraq's superweapons programme had been seized at Heathrow airport in a sting operation by British and American intelligence officers. The seizure of the nuclear triggers, in the wake of Farzad's hanging, added to the growing world-wide unease at the Iraqi regime. The Iraqis were angry.

At 5.31 a.m. Chilean time on 31 March 1990, Moyle called his fiancée. At 5.36 a.m. he called his parents. Tony Moyle told *Newsnight* that he was in very high spirits, but Jonathan closed the call by saying that he had started feeling very tired.

Two hours later the chambermaid collected the laundry. She recollected later that the safety chain was off the door, which was unusual for Moyle. (This tells us immediately that Moyle, a fit, 28-year-old, had reason to be anxious about his personal security. Readers who have followed the story of the Iraqis' promiscuous use of assassination thus far would agree that Moyle was right.) She came back to the room at 9.30 a.m. to collect bed-linen. She saw a bloodstain 9 to 12 inches long on the sheet. Once she had finished, she opened the clothes closet to find the suspended body. *The Times* reported on 30 May 1990: 'His 5 ft 8 ins body was found hanging from a clothes rail 5 ft off the ground in a cupboard with the door closed from the outside.' At the post mortem, the Chilean pathologist found traces of diazepam, a powerful sedative, in his stomach.

Remember the Defence Intelligence Staff report which stated: 'The amount of assistance that "UK Ltd", in particular our machinery manufacturers, are giving to Iraq towards the set-up of a major arms R&D and production industry' represented 'a very significant enhancement to the ability of Iraq to manufacture its own arms . . . All it needs is for an investigative journalist to pull together the threads.'

Whitehall need not have worried. Journalists investigating Iraq's arms procurement network did not have a very long lifespan.

In between the deaths of the two reporters, an assassin had gunned down Dr Bull, the inventor of the supergun, on 22 March 1990, outside the door of his Belgian flat. The killer had fired two bullets into the back of his neck and pumped three more into his corpse, using a Colt automatic fitted with a silencer. The Belgian police found $20,000 untouched in Dr Bull's wallet. The killer was not interested in loose change.

The Iraqi arms procurement network was beginning to look

like, in one of Saddam's pet phrases, a 'lake of blood'. Before the year was out the lake would get bloodier. One would have thought that the British government would have had enough. Instead, it plunged in even deeper.

CHAPTER
NINE

Savour – as the corpses piled up – the following letter from Lord Trefgarne, dated 30 March 1990, to Waldegrave. It is an epic of expediency. Headlined: 'Iraq: outstanding export licence applications for machine tool exports', Trefgarne was pressing for yet more Matrix Churchill machine tools to go to Iraq. He wrote that ministers had agreed, on 1 November 1989, to approve a batch of Matrix Churchill machine tools for Iraq

in the knowledge that Iraq was seeking to acquire technology for CW [chemical weapons] and for ballistic missile operations . . . There is no evidence to suggest that the current exports are for anything other than for general engineering. In December, of course, Iraq was reported to have launched a ballistic missile. This was only to be expected . . . [The missile launch may not have surprised Trefgarne, but it scared the pants off Iraq's enemies.] Neither do I think Wednesday's discovery of illegal exports of nuclear trigger devices alters the case for approval. Iraq's nuclear ambitions have been known for some time . . . It would be wrong to close this significant market to our machine tool manufacturers who are facing strong European competition in Iraq and elsewhere.

The market was God. The trade with Iraq must go on.

In April Saddam threatened the fragile peace of the Middle East. He declared: 'I swear to God, we will let our fire consume

175

half of Israel if it tries to wage anything against Iraq.' It was discounted as Baathist rhetoric, but it turned out to be half the Iraqi government's foreign policy, the other half being the invasion of Kuwait. That month, at long last, an arm of the British government entered the lists to fight the good fight with some conviction. Her Majesty's Customs and Excise pounced on some long tubes at Middlesbrough docks. After an amusing argy-bargy over whether they really were part of an oil pipeline, the Customs men satisfied themselves the parts were for Iraq's supergun and impounded the lot. It was the first bloody nose for Britain's hitherto untouched Iraq lobby.

Even in 1990, Iraq still had people prepared to see its point of view. The US State Department had castigated Iraq in its 1989 country-by-country human rights reports; the Amnesty International folder is just too sickening to read; Mrs Thatcher herself had condemned Iraqi 'barbarism'. But in the House of Commons debate on the supergun affair, Richard Page, the Tory MP who met Saddam on the trip to Iraq in 1988, defended the Iraqis for trying 'to bypass an arms embargo'. His speech prompted a cynical question from Labour member David Winnick: 'How much was the Honourable Gentleman paid?' Page replied: 'I am paid by no government and no government agency.' He made no mention of the free fudge.

There was one puzzling aspect to the supergun debate and its aftermath. Foreign secretary Hurd wrote to his Labour shadow, Gerald Kaufman: 'We did not learn of the involvement of British companies in supplying tubes for the Iraqi long range gun (or supergun) project until 30 March 1990.' This statement appears to conflict with the 27 October 1989 intelligence report, when a British businessman, Henderson, was said to have passed over supergun blueprints to MI6, who reported to Hurd.

The Foreign Office's revulsion at Farzad's execution was softening by the day. On 2 April 1990, Waldegrave wrote to Tom Sackville, MP, giving a tough signal of diplomatic disdain: 'We were appalled . . . reacted vigorously to this dreadful news . . . a series of measures which we have taken to make clear our disgust at the Iraqi reaction . . .'

Three days later, the line was showing a wobble. In a statement to the House of Commons, the minister said:

> There is no question of isolating Iraq. The Arab League unanimously supports Iraq on the Bazoft case . . . Therefore, I fear that it is being hopeful to have ideas that cutting off British trade credits and trying to prevent British businessmen from going to the market – not that we could legally do it – would isolate Iraq. That could create satisfaction among our industrial competitors and it would lose us jobs and orders in Britain. It would have no other effect.

Waldegrave wrote back to Trefgarne on 30 May 1990, asking for a three-month hold on the question of approving or not a new batch of machine tools 'when the interest generated by the supergun may have subsided'. Given the heap of bodies, the nuclear triggers which were seized at Heathrow, the bits of the supergun rusting on Middlesbrough docks, what is most striking about Waldegrave's letter is the apologetic fashion in which he calls for the delay. He conceded to Trefgarne: 'We do not have incontrovertible evidence to suggest that the machinery in question will be used for anything but legitimate civil purposes.'

This was a strange concession. A sharper Foreign Office letter to the DTI might have gone something like this:

> We know that British and American intelligence believe that some Matrix Churchill machine tools are making ammunitions; have done so since 1987. We know that Western intelligence believe that the Iraqis are using a Cardoen factory to make chemical weapons. We know that Habobi, cited as head of the Iraqi arms procurement network by British intelligence, is head of the Nassir factory. We know that the Habobi ring is shopping for nuclear technology. We know that Saddam has recently threatened to 'let our fire consume half of Israel'. In the last few years, he has repeatedly carried out his worst threats, e.g. Halabja, the 1988 summer gassing of the Kurds, the execution of a British-based journalist, Farzad Bazoft.

Given everything we know about Iraq's arms procurement network and how the Baathist state works, it is absurd that the DTI should accept any Iraqi claims that the goods are for peaceful uses. In the light of the above evidence, allowing more machine tools to go to Iraq is imprudent.

It is puzzling that Waldegrave chose to be so pussy-footed in his choice of language.

Concession to the DTI granted, Waldegrave emphasized not the moral but the presentational problems if the new batch of machine tools went ahead:

The nuclear capacitors and supergun problems have generated a very high level of interest in parliament and the media in the supply of high technology equipment to Iraq ... In present circumstances I believe the government would be strongly criticized if we allowed the export of machine tools which could be used on the supergun or related projects, particularly given Matrix's links with SRC [the late Dr Bull's firm, makers of the supergun]. We would, with some justification, be accused of being ... irresponsible. Douglas Hurd has seen this letter and agrees.

You may care to note that whereas Sir Geoffrey Howe before and Douglas Hurd after are mentioned fairly frequently in the Matrix Churchill documents – because the foreign secretary is such a key player in the Whitehall game – the man between the two, John Major, is not at all.

Alan Clark also was not over-anxious to proceed. He wrote to Trefgarne on 3 May 1990:

In the light of other developments since your letter, however, you may wish to give further consideration as to whether this is the right time ... The Cabinet Office are at present co-ordinating the handling of presentational aspects of government actions in relation to the Iraqi [super] gun and you may wish to inform them ...

Meanwhile, the ECGD men were not resting. The Matrix Churchill documents show that Alex Mayne Reid of the ECGD ordered a transcription of an ITN bulletin on 30 May 1990, which broke new ground on the death of defence journalist Jonathan Moyle. ITN's Ian Williams reported that a fresh police inquiry had unearthed new evidence on the death. He said: 'A chambermaid now says she overheard a heated argument, in English, as she passed Moyle's door, late on the evening before his death.

'When the room was cleaned the following morning, a maid now says she found a bloodstain the size of a hand on the sheets. And files were missing from the room, according to the investigating judge. Staff now say that someone called a taxi for Moyle around six in the morning, the time he's thought to have died. An hour earlier, they say, a foreigner was pacing anxiously in the lobby . . . In Chile, British authorities are encouraging the theory that Moyle's death was suicide. That looks increasingly unlikely.'

The ECGD also clipped a photocopy of an article in the *Independent on Sunday*, dated 20 June 1990, on Moyle's death, with the note scribbled in hand: 'Please attach to buyer file – Chile: Cardoen Industrias.'

Moyle's parents might be heartened to know that at least one branch of the British government made it their business to be aware of the suspicions about their son's death. The newspaper article by Tim Kelsey reported:

> On the night before his death, Mr Moyle had an argument in his room with another man, according to a chambermaid. At 5 a.m. the next morning, said the hotel reception, the man booked a taxi in the name of Mr Moyle and left.
>
> It has been alleged that Raul Montesino, press officer with Cardoen, was the other man, but he denies this.

It was Montesino who denied to the *Financial Times* on 1 November 1988 the belief of 'Western intelligence sources' that Cardoen was making a munitions factory where the Iraqis were building chemical weapons.

The strange circumstances surrounding the death of Jonathan Moyle were finally beginning to attract media attention, despite the government-sponsored briefings pointing to the suicide theory. There was one more corpse to add to the heap of bodies connected with trade with Iraq that summer, in a story little noticed by Fleet Street. One of the jewels of British democracy is the local newspapers, who record in commendable detail the doings of would-be local politicians. Take the 3 May 1990 Nuneaton and Bedworth *Herald and Post* newspaper. Its headline screamed: 'My Iraq Job By Tory Gordon'. The story by reporter Mike Malyon read:

> A Tory candidate in today's borough council elections will miss the hustings action because of work commitments in Iraq. But Gordon Glass, who is standing for Coton Ward, has denied the machinery he is installing in a factory near Baghdad is for the Iraqi arms industry. Mr Glass, who left yesterday for a three-week contract, had to arrange his own vote by proxy. He said: 'I will be with a team of service engineers installing machinery in a factory in Iraq. It is my second visit and I am working as a sub-contractor for Matrix Churchill Ltd.'

The *Herald and Post* reminded readers that Matrix Churchill had been named in the national press as allegedly supplying machinery to Iraq for the production of mortar shells. It went on to quote 58-year-old Glass: 'We are installing machines for slide-grinding, plane-milling and jig-boring. They cannot be used in the armaments industry. I am not saying that the machine could not be adapted for such use. But, as far as I am aware, the equipment in the factory I am working at is not used for making any sorts of weapons or mortars.'

A British engineer installing Matrix Churchill machines with Glass in Iraq took a different view. In a letter the engineer described the scene:

'It was obviously a munitions factory. The main gates were guarded by at least 25 to 30 soldiers, all armed with automatic weapons. The surrounding areas were guarded by surface-to-air missile launchers, manned by a five-strong squad. Everywhere I looked there were large and small rockets, again with missile launchers. The ground was littered with spent shells.'

Herald and Post reporter Malyon was one of the last people in Britain to speak to Glass, who did not win election to the council. On 24 May 1990 Malyon reported in the paper: 'Iraq Tragedy: New Riddle.' The story explained how Glass had died in his hotel room in Baghdad, two days after being mugged. Iraqi police attention had for no good reason focused on the man who found the body, another British expatriate worker, Simon Brogan, who was shocked and terrified. The paper added: 'The mystery deepened when the *Herald and Post* tried to contact him [Brogan] at his hotel. An Englishman answered the phone and said: "You should not have called me." Another English voice came on the line and said: "He cannot speak to anyone." The line was then cut off.'

On 31 May 1990 the *Herald and Post* reported on Brogan's 'Nightmare in Baghdad'. Malyon reported: 'Brogan, 30, said: "I was the last person to see Gordon alive and I was the one who found his body. And I suddenly had the awful feeling that I was under suspicion. I was very scared. The circumstances of the death were a mystery and I was in the middle of a lot of intense questioning. I had fearful thoughts of the police coming to arrest me in the middle of the night and I could not sleep."' Glass had been bruised and cut in the mugging, but had appeared to have fully recovered, and had had a drink in the bar on the night before his death, the paper reported. Brogan was arrested by the Iraqi police, but had the presence of mind to call for an official from the British embassy. His passport was confiscated and Brogan was called before an Iraqi judge: '"I was shaking like a leaf."' Eventually, he was freed and put on the plane home. At Birmingham airport, he was met by police and escorted through a side door to a waiting car.

He added: '"Gordon was a smashing bloke and a real friend. His death was upsetting enough and all that business afterwards only made things worse."'

The paper reported that the pair had gone to Iraq for a

three-week business trip, under contract to Matrix Churchill. Brogan found the body of his friend three days before they were due to return home.

On 30 August 1990 the paper reported that the Nuneaton Coroner Allan Dixon heard that Glass had suffered two previous collapses, but lacked a full post-mortem report from the Iraqis. The coroner determined an open verdict.

The story of the death of Glass received scant attention from the rest of Fleet Street. The *Independent* had reported the death on 18 May 1990, in a three-paragraph story sourcing the news item to the Foreign Office. The report closed: 'Mr Glass, of Nuneaton, Warwickshire, was working for the Coventry engineering firm Graham Johnson, installing machine tools in a factory.'

Had the Foreign Office briefing on the death pointed out that Glass was a sub-contractor working for Iraqi-owned Matrix Churchill installing machine tools in a munitions factory, then the story of a mystery killing of a British engineer might perhaps have had greater prominence. The magic words 'Matrix Churchill' would have been enough to get antennae twitching. It is, of course, very likely that Glass died of natural causes brought on by the mugging. However, the firm '"He cannot speak to anyone"' reply to the local newspaper's enquiries, the hush-hush way Brogan was spirited back to Britain and 'escorted through a side door' of Birmingham airport and the economical Foreign Office briefing suggest that the British government was anxious not to cast any unnecessary light on Matrix Churchill's business in Iraq.

From June 1990 onwards the Iraqgate scandal begins to unravel, with journalists and the Duty men from Customs and Excise digging up more and more unappetizing bones. The DTI were starting to get twitchy. Civil servant Michael Coolican's memo on 14 June 1990, to Nicholas Ridley, secretary of state for trade and industry, catches the increasingly frantic mood beautifully. It has been quoted in part earlier, but you may well appreciate the quality of its frenzy:

Customs have *prima facie* evidence that current machine tools exports from Matrix Churchill and other UK companies under licence are being routed via Chile to Iraq for arms manufacture. Evidence was available in 1987 to the same effect, but to protect sources ministers took a decision to let the exports go ahead. An investigation will clearly bring all these to light . . . Are ministers willing to have the 1987 and subsequent decisions exposed and made the subject of court room argument? . . . The dirty washing liable to emerge from the action proposed by Customs will add to the problems posed by the [super] gun. For the DTI, the timing is extraordinarily embarrassing.

Waldegrave's blood was up. On 19 June 1990 he wrote a letter to Trefgarne rehearsing all the arguments in favour of postponing any decision on the new batch of machine tools for three months. He wrote:

Although we have no incontrovertible proof that the equipment in question will be used in arms manufacture, the overall intelligence picture suggests that it might well. If, as seems likely, there are further revelations about indigenous Iraqi arms manufacture and Matrix Churchill are again implicated, we would, entirely justifiably in my view, be sharply criticized for approving such licences. We could not argue that we had not been adequately warned.

Although it is not possible for us to prevent the governments of other friendly potential supplier countries from allowing the sale by their own companies of similar equipment to Iraq, we would be happy to inform such countries that we are not intending to do so, giving our reasons.

Sharp-eyed readers will have spotted that this 19 June 1990 Waldegrave letter argues a case 180 degrees opposite to the 5 April 1990 Waldegrave speech to the House of Commons.

Yet another facet of the twinkling prism of the Waldegrave persona was on show that summer, a few days before the invasion of Kuwait, when he showed up at an al fresco barbecue. The host? The Kurdish community? The democratic opposition to

Saddam? The BBC's *Panorama* camera caught the minister chatting amiably to the host. The television film reveals that 'one of the series of measures which we have taken to make clear our disgust at the Iraqi action' over the hanging of Farzad was to go to the Iraqi ambassador's summer party. Half hidden behind someone's glass of bubbly, is that . . .? Could it be . . . Lord Trefgarne? The glimpse is too fleeting to be sure. Did Waldegrave use the social opportunity to bring up the question of Farzad's execution? Was he 'appalled? Did he react vigorously . . . this dreadful news . . .' etc. Up to a point. He told the ambassador about how 'my sister used to own this house' and to others offered more chit-chat about looking forward to his summer holiday: 'I'm rather counting the days.' The minister's gift to the language of expediency will be his 'screwdrivers . . .' maxim. One could improve on it, by changing one word: 'Waldegraves are also required to make nuclear bombs.'

The nearest thing to a primal scream on paper landed on Number 10's doormat on 21 June 1990. The day before trade secretary Ridley wrote to Customs and Excise, letting them know that he was going to write to the prime minister about 'Exports to Iraq'. The letter was copied to the private secretary of the chancellor, John Major. He has said he didn't see it.

The next day came the primal scream. Ridley wrote to the prime minister, clearly fearing that the balloon was about to go up. It already had. Three Customs officers arrived at the Matrix Churchill offices in Coventry the same day, requiring to see copies of their contracts with Iraq.

The contents of Ridley's special pleading with the prime minister reveal much about the hidden policy of the British government towards Iraq. He wrote:

Customs and Excise have received information (from West German Customs) suggesting that Matrix Churchill (part Iraqi owned) exported machine tools to Chile which were onsold to Iraq and used for munitions manufacture, and that they and other companies exported machine tools to Iraq direct for that purpose, despite furnishing statements that the equipment was required for general engineering purposes.

Relations [with Iraq] are of course already strained. Following our action to intercept shipments of parts of the big gun and the nuclear triggers, the Iraqi Ministry of Industry and Military Manufacturing, which accounts for around 60 per cent of Iraqi industrial procurement, announced that trade with the UK was under review . . . I wrote to the Iraqi minister to assure him of our wish for normal commercial relations with Iraq . . . Our ambassador delivered my letter at a call on the Iraqi minister last week. The Iraqi minister's response was not reassuring . . . The minister is the President's son-in-law and a member of the inner circle of the regime.

Consider the implied sycophancy of the letter to Hussein Kamil; the use of the ambassador as a sort of gilded postman. This was another signal going to Baghdad; one which made a nonsense of the public talk of ministers' disgust at Iraqi 'barbarity'.

The beef of Ridley's letter is to be had in one sentence of seven words: 'ECGD's exposure in Iraq is £1 billion.' Ridley went on: 'A further £250 million was offered and accepted at the Joint Commission Meeting last November . . . the present high level of arrears reflects the cessation of payments during the last two months or so which was evidently linked with the current political coolness . . .'

Ridley went on to call for a 'more thorough review of our policy in this area'. The letter was copied to members of the OD committee – Cabinet Overseas and Defence Committee – of which the then chancellor, John Major, was a member.

That policy review took place on 19 July 1990, with foreign secretary Hurd in the chair. The chancellor perhaps would have expected to be present – but Major has said he wasn't there. The latest batch of Matrix Churchill machine tools was destined for a shell-making factory and a rocket artillery project.

At that 19 July 1990 meeting the ministers let the machine tools go.

This astonishing turn of events can be deduced from a letter to Matrix Churchill from the DTI, dated 29 July 1990, and a phone call between Henderson and Coolican on 1 August 1990. Henderson told *Panorama* (broadcast on 23 November 1992): 'On the first of August, I actually telephoned Michael Coolican at the Department of Trade and Industry regarding a number of licences that were outstanding both for Matrix Churchill and other companies, and during that conversation he informed me that all the licences had now been cleared except for five machines which were to be imported from the USA.'

The tanks rolled into Kuwait before dawn the next day.

It was everybody's fault. It was nobody's fault. It really was very embarrassing. All those meals Ford had eaten at the taxpayers' expense, jotting down intelligence from Gutteridge. All those minutes – albeit completely blacked out – from Henderson's spying. All those Matrix Churchill machine tools cluttering up Saddam's munitions factories, waiting to be discovered by the UN investigators. All those clever equivocations. The 'but no conclusive' line on the gassing of the Kurds. The leak to the *Sun* of Farzad's past. The eagerly accepted suicide verdict on Jonathan Moyle. All those dead bodies. All that kowtowing. All that trading with the enemy. It really was very, very embarrassing.

Even before the invasion, Whitehall started to line up the alibis, as smoothly as the Norman Stanley Fletcher character played by Ronnie Barker in *Porridge*. It wasn't me, guv – it was 'intelligence'.

A senior officer in British intelligence, whose name has been blacked out, pounced on that alibi on 24 July 1990. The recipient of his letter was D. J. C. Ball, Esq., of the Cabinet Office. The spook scolded:

Paragraph 8 states that 'Ministers have allowed the supply of some Matrix Churchill machine tools, for ad hoc reasons of an intelligence nature'.

As I read it, the implication of this is that 'intelligence' considerations influenced ministers to allow exports of machine tools from Matrix Churchill, and without such considerations, no such exports would have been permitted. Assuming that the 'intelligence' connection refers to our own activities, I think it worth placing on record that our understanding of the situation is somewhat different.

The spook pointed out that although there were reservations

about a proposal to take action against Matrix Churchill in the context of its exports of machine tools to Iraq, on the grounds that it might compromise our operational interest in the matter . . . we later withdrew our reservations . . . and made it clear . . . we had no objection to departments taking whatever actions they might think fit . . .

If the story of the secret trade got out, it would be very embarrassing.

Henderson, Abraham and Allen were arrested on 16 October 1990. The effect of the arrests was threefold: it dampened all subsequent journalistic investigation of Matrix Churchill until after the case had come to court because of fears of breaking the *sub judice* rules of British justice; it gave the government a reason to say nothing, also for fear of breaching *sub judice*; it caused MI6 to drop their agent. Henderson told Thames Television's *This Week*, broadcast on 19 November 1992: 'After my arrest I did try to contact them by telephone, but my calls were never ever returned.'

The heat started to build on the Iraqgate scandal. On 2 December 1990, the *Sunday Times* ran a story based on the machine tool makers' recollection of the meeting with Alan Clark in January 1988. The story quoted Henderson as saying: 'Everybody knew the machines could make shells . . . The minister was giving us a nod and a wink.'

Clark was not a happy man. He told reporters hanging about outside Downing Street: 'I have never given a nod and a wink to anybody. The whole thing is highly defamatory.'

In early December Tim Sainsbury trotted out the familiar

party line to the House of Commons: 'The guidelines are clear. They were set out in 1985 and since then have been scrupulously and carefully followed in the issue of licences. No other country has such a careful method for scrutinizing applications for export licences and for controlling exports.'

The accidental utility of the Matrix Churchill arrests came immediately into play. In early December 1990 Major was taken to task by Liberal leader Paddy Ashdown on his part in the affair. Major gave a dry-as-dust answer. After the release of the Matrix Churchill documents, Ashdown wrote to Major on 11 November 1992, claiming that the prime minister had misled him by concealing knowledge of the case. Major replied on 12 November 1992:

> If you read my letter [of 6 December 1990] you will see that I refer, in the second paragraph, to an investigation by HM Customs and Excise, an investigation which was into Matrix Churchill. I made it clear I could not comment in case I prejudiced any proceedings. That then is the 'rational explanation' which you have asked for: that you have failed to understand our earlier correspondence.

In fact, since the Matrix Churchill arrests, there has been a constant problem that ministers might 'prejudice any proceedings', a problem solved by declining to comment: first with the Matrix Churchill case, and, now, with the inquiry headed by Lord Justice Scott.

There was a short gap when Iraqgate was not covered in some way by legal proceedings, and in that gap Radio Four's *PM* programme could find no minister to answer questions. After that gap, all the ministers from Major to Newton have been able to reply to any troubling question: 'That is a matter for the Scott inquiry.'

The story rumbled on, with the odd twist and turn. In America, President Bush found that he could not play the triumphant commander-in-chief card as hard as he had wished, because diligent investigation showed that his administration had conspired in the arming of the enemy prior to the second Gulf War. Iraqgate was one reason why Bush lost to Clinton. However, the prospect of the Matrix Churchill trial diffused much of the Iraqgate heat in Britain. The story of how UK Ltd did its bit to arm the Butcher of Baghdad was not an issue in the British general election.

Eventually, in September 1992, the arthritic plod of the law caught up with Iraqgate. The defence of the Matrix Churchill Three set out to get discovery of the secret documents which showed how much Whitehall and ministers had conspired in the arming of Iraq. Whitehall fought hard. Four ministers signed Public Interest Immunity Certificates, declaring that the secrets must stay secret. Tristan Garel-Jones, MP, the minister of state at the Foreign Office, Kenneth Clarke, president of the Board of Trade, Michael Heseltine and defence secretary Malcolm Rifkind all signed on the dotted line, arguing that national security was at stake.

Judge Brian Smedley read the documents. He disagreed. The defence got discovery and the Crown's case was sunk from the word go.

One aspect of the Public Interest Immunity Certificates caused former Labour shadow foreign secretary Gerald Kaufman to invoke Sherlock Holmes. He wrote in the *Guardian* on 23 November 1992:

> Douglas Hurd, the Secretary of State in charge of the arms embargo, has uttered not a syllable. While in other departments the Public Interest Immunity Certificates were signed by the relevant Secretaries of State, Hurd left it to his subordinate, Garel-Jones, to sign for the Foreign Office.
>
> 'Is there any point to which you would wish to draw my attention?'
>
> 'To the curious incident of the dog in the night-time.'
>
> 'The dog did nothing in the night-time.'
>
> 'That was the curious incident,' remarked Sherlock Holmes.'

CHAPTER
TEN

Remember the House of Dolls.

Beneath the blank spectacles of the John Major doll lies the imperious, all-knowing stare of Margaret, now Lady Thatcher.

Beneath the Thatcher doll lies the foreign secretary, Douglas Hurd, the doll who didn't bark.

Beneath the Hurd doll lies David Mellor, who sat with Saddam on a sofa, and later praised Iraq's national health service – which kills its victims by draining them of their blood.

Beneath the Mellor doll lies Tony Newton, now leader of the House of Commons, who doubled the trade credits for the Iraqi killers after the gassing of Halabja.

Beneath the Newton doll lies former trade and industry secretary Peter Lilley, whose department allowed the shipment of chemicals to make gases which could kill the Kurds.

Beneath the Lilley doll lies John, now Lord Wakeham, of the House of Lords, who went to Baghdad in 1989 to talk trade with the Iraqis' while they were holding a British journalist, whom they later hanged.

Beneath the Wakeham doll lies William Waldegrave, who twice condemned the barbarities of Iraq, then went to the summer party of the Iraqi ambassador.

Beneath the Waldegrave doll lies trade secretary Nicholas Ridley, who didn't want to upset the Iraqis lest they not pay up. (They didn't.)

Beneath the Ridley doll lies the opaque spectacles of Lord Trefgarne, who promoted the secret trade.

Beneath Trefgarne lies Alan Clark, the doll who told the truth and was made a scapegoat.

Beneath Clark lies Sarah, Duchess of York, who welcomed one of Saddam's men to dinner at Buckingham Palace.

Beneath the Duchess doll lies a freebie of MPs, clutching bits of steam engines, cheap mugs and Iraqi fudge.

Beneath the MP dolls lie five minister dolls who tried to cover up the secret trade 'in the national interest' but at some risk of sending the Matrix Churchill Three to prison: attorney general Sir Nicholas Lyell, who advised the others that they could sign that the secrets should stay secret; president of the Board of Trade Michael Heseltine, who raged at 'nauseating hypocrisy'; junior Foreign Office minister Tristan Garel-Jones, who had to sign because his master, foreign secretary Hurd, could not; defence secretary Malcolm Rifkind, who saw danger to the national interest if the truth came out; home secretary Kenneth Clarke, who was behind with his reading.

Beneath Clarke was a battery of leading civil servants, who conspired to the effect that the secret trade was kept secret.

Beneath the civil servant dolls lie the faceless officers of MI5 and MI6.

And beneath them all lies Saddam, laughing at the lot.

Many of the scandals illuminated in this book will, necessarily, be examined by Lord Justice Scott's inquiry. It is hard to think where the poor man will start: our supplying of munitions-making tools to the Iraqis? Our paying for those tools? Our covering up of that supply? Our dissembling over Saddam's use of poison gas so that we did not lose his business? Our crocodile tears at the death of thousands of Kurds? Our arming of Iraq?

It is hard to imagine how some of the Cabinet ministers central to this story can stay in office once the public realizes the full majesty of what they did. Major, Clarke, Heseltine, Hurd, Lamont, Lilley, Lyell, Mellor (gone for the moment but there is always the chance of a comeback), Newton, Rifkind, Wakeham,

Waldegrave: they all knew something of the trade and some of them tried to cover it up.

One should reserve a special admiration for those who went to Baghdad and furthered trade with our enemy after Halabja: Mellor, Newton, Wakeham, Waldegrave. Not forgetting the two chief secretaries who insured the trade: Major and Lamont.

The individual dolls leer and pout in their own separate ways but together, as a set of dolls, they speak eloquently to a culture which placed commerce above common humanity.

Exhausted with the evidence of expediency, sickened by the incompetence that led us to miss the invasion of Kuwait, brutalized by the cynical looking-away from horror, one emotion alone prevails that my country armed a tyrant so cruel as Saddam.

Shame.

Index